THE AGILE CODEX

RE-INVENTING AGILE THROUGH THE SCIENCE OF INVENTION AND ASSEMBLY

Michael McCormick

Apress®

The Agile Codex: Re-inventing Agile Through the Science of Invention and Assembly

Michael McCormick
Boulder, CO, USA

ISBN-13 (pbk): 978-1-4842-7279-4   ISBN-13 (electronic): 978-1-4842-7280-0
https://doi.org/10.1007/978-1-4842-7280-0

Managing Director, Apress Media LLC: Welmoed Spahr
Acquisitions Editor: Shiva Ramachandran
Development Editor: Matthew Moodie
Coordinating Editor: Jessica Vakili

Distributed to the book trade worldwide by Springer Science+Business Media New York, 1 New York Plaza, New York, NY 100043. Phone 1-800-SPRINGER, fax (201) 348-4505, e-mail orders-ny@springer-sbm.com, or visit www.springeronline.com. Apress Media, LLC is a California LLC and the sole member (owner) is Springer Science + Business Media Finance Inc (SSBM Finance Inc). SSBM Finance Inc is a **Delaware** corporation.

For information on translations, please e-mail booktranslations@springernature.com; for reprint, paperback, or audio rights, please e-mail bookpermissions@springernature.com.

Apress titles may be purchased in bulk for academic, corporate, or promotional use. eBook versions and licenses are also available for most titles. For more information, reference our Print and eBook Bulk Sales web page at http://www.apress.com/bulk-sales.

Any source code or other supplementary material referenced by the author in this book is available to readers on GitHub via the book's product page, located at www.apress.com/978-1-4842-7279-4. For more detailed information, please visit http://www.apress.com/source-code.

Printed on acid-free paper

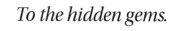

To the hidden gems.

Contents

About the Author. vii

Part I: The Accident I
Chapter 1:   Clear Ownership. 5
Chapter 2:   Small, Independent Units of Work. 15
Chapter 3:   Sized. 25
Chapter 4:   Sequenced 29
Chapter 5:   Inputs, Transition Criteria, Outputs. 33
Chapter 6:   Stakeholder Approval 37

Part II: The Agile Codex Theory. 41
Chapter 7:   The Problem 45
Chapter 8:   The Codex 51
Chapter 9:   The Agile. 57
Chapter 10: Benefits. 61
Chapter 11: From Invention to Assembly Line 65
Chapter 12: Team Functions. 77
Chapter 13: Software Development Life Cycle. 79
Chapter 14: Risk Management. 87

Part III: The Agile Codex Practice. 99
Chapter 15: Building Blocks 101
Chapter 16: Workflow 107
Chapter 17: Metrics. 135
Chapter 18: Teaching the Teams 143
Chapter 19: What Next? 147
Conclusion. 153

Index. 155

About the Author

Michael McCormick is VP of Software Engineering at Salesforce. Michael holds several engineering patents in mobile, IoT, and microservices systems design and wrote a top 10 iPhone app (Photography, 2011). A lover of language, Michael knows English, Spanish, French, German, Norwegian, and a little bit of Hindi. A composer of music, he plays classical and electric guitar, bass, and piano, and he has also been known to sing. With his family, he enjoys playing music, strategy card games, biking, playing outside, traveling, reading out loud, and watching 1980s movies. Michael values finding the hidden gems and turning disparate skill sets into creative innovation.

The Accident

Introduction

Sometimes you need something to completely break before you realize how many pieces went into it. And seeing what those pieces actually are gives you a chance to understand it in an entirely different, deeper way. From this atomized state, you have ultimate flexibility in how you put it back together, and ultimate visibility to all the possible combinations. There are no preconceived notions. No pre-assembled bits. Just a knowledge of what the thing needs to do once you put it back together.

That was my situation. I had been given a software development project and team in crisis. This product was promised to customers. This product was promised to internal enablement teams. In three months. The project and team were completely broken.

Like a first responder arriving at an accident scene, I had urgent triage to do on the victims.

I interviewed each developer. I scoured the Jira project and design documents. This is what I learned.

The project had been handed to a few senior developers by a senior executive via a set of gap-filled verbal summary descriptions of the vision, heard slightly differently each time. A product manager, who was over-allocated, had made a best effort in his free time to spread his inferences of the senior executive's vision, dosed with some practical reality and his own opinions as well, across a dozen Epics in Jira, usually with a single line such as "Give end user ability to view activity" or what could best be characterized as a to-do: "Admin experience."

The handful of developers were left to float for a few months, drawing up design documents and continuing the lines of inference down to the User Story level. They spent some time writing code, spiking, coming up with questions, getting unspecific answers, and then just moving forward with whatever made the most sense to them at the time.

Then, in an effort to "speed delivery," a dozen more developers were added to the team, and the engineering manager was quickly overwhelmed as he still had two other teams to manage. The engineering manager delegated scrum master duties to one of the original core developers and largely disappeared from daily interactions with the team. The newly ordained scrum master started all the sprint rituals with the new team, from daily standups to retrospectives. There was still no full-time product manager.

With increasing pressure to provide a commitment to the pre-ordained delivery date, they did their best to figure out what they were trying to build. Each developer took ownership of an Epic and, feeling the pressure, sized them optimistically, sometimes predicting completion in as little as a week, without time to study the code or plan the design.

They plunged forward, working on Epics with few or no User Stories, delivering code as a best guess for what they needed to do. If there were a User Story or two, they were also one-liners, and not sized. They were brought into existence just before they were needed or, if earlier, they were abandoned or forgotten, because the project had no backlog set up. Much work was done without any User Story to track it at all.

Labels were created and applied to categorize the state of or grouping of a story, and as those things changed, the labels did not. Each developer had their own interpretation of what many of the labels actually indicated. Reports were created to give metrics to the labels, and as they drifted out of functional usefulness, they were abandoned but not removed.

Many Epics contained User Stories that seemed to no longer apply to the Epic. Duplicate User Stories seemed to exist, with subjects like "Logging implementation for users" and "User logging." User Stories implied and referred to, but did not link to, designs that did not exist in any identifiable location.

There was no backlog. There was no plan for sequencing and tracking work, or predicting when it would be completed, except for a spreadsheet of Epics and owners and sizing which was used during standups to update on progress toward Epic completion.

No matter how much time a developer spent on the work, at every standup the amount of estimated time left to complete the work was the same. If estimates changed, there would be challenges and lectures from senior management. Having to plan or detail, the developers could not respond with any organized story, justifications, or nuance. Senior management bullied them into hiding their confusion. Every day, the update was the same, lots of work was done, progress was made, and the amount of work remaining stayed the same.

The architectural design documentation drifted out of date. The evolved intentions remained in the heads of the original developers who had been too busy writing quickly pivoting code. These developers were also too busy to answer the questions posed by the new developers, who then made their own assumptions.

Code was written, overwritten, rewritten, by multiple people in the same areas, acting independently and simultaneously. Feature branches were open for weeks, then sent for a rubber stamp review and disruptive merge conflict with a constant stream of quality regressions in their wake. Even finding out if a product behavior was intentional and desired or a bug in need of a fix often required a lengthy round trip with a product manager who was not paying enough attention to give a consistent or thorough answer, if an answer came at all.

No one knew whom to ask their questions. Messages to the team would sit, eternally unanswered. Sometimes they were answered one-to-one, in order to avoid appearing responsible for providing the answer should it prove too difficult to come up with.

Eventually, people stopped asking questions at all.

As the team grew, the Jira board became a dumping ground of cross-team to-do lists. Product managers, UX designers, QE, operations: all using the same project board to track their work. Developer User Stories started accumulating tasks which were owned not only by multiple developers but also by people in other teams.

A backlog appeared. Some User Stories in the backlog had tasks that were complete because they were needed by another task in a story that was being actively worked on. Other tasks in the backlog story could not start until a story ahead of that one could be completed.

Developers found it so confusing to track their work in Jira this way that they began neglecting the tickets, and Jira's representation of it, as a source of truth. User Stories that were complete were still in backlog. What a Story said was being delivered to test was completely different from the reality. User Stories that were complete were often only partially complete. User Stories languished on the board as a task stayed incomplete, waiting on a cross-team contributor who had lost track or did not know the priority or state of the work well enough to do their part.

Throughout the User Stories' life cycle, deviations from design were not documented, so no one knew if they were the result of accidents or conversations. The UX team repeatedly had to disclaim deliveries as the senior executives railed against poor design.

No one felt empowered or any sense of ownership – just a dreadful sense of accountability to figure out how to deliver a thing they did not understand on an arbitrary date. Even the most benevolent on the team became habituated to find fault in how another team or person had let them down, blocked them, and kept them from delivering and doing their part. The teams were helpless, defensive, confused, and on constant high alert, getting more pressure and taking more shortcuts by the day.

I was thrown right into the middle of this resource and leadership vacuum. With the luxury of having had no hand in the downward spiral, and nowhere to go but up, I had nothing to lose and nothing to break.

The first section of this book details my path to triaging this project, team, and product back to life, and the unique Agile principles and processes I uncovered along the way – principles I would not have been able to see so clearly had I not been handed a project so completely decimated.

The second section of this book reflects on the principles from an academic and scientific standpoint, drawing on modern organizational theory and the industrial age science of the assembly line, providing a template for how to develop and apply them to improve your own Agile processes, no matter what the current state of your project.

While Agile is a broad enough term that it can be difficult to point at any one thing and say "that is" or "that is not" Agile without someone having a contrary opinion, I do commit some clear Agile blasphemy, for as my experience shows, some things need to be broken to be fixed.

Clear Ownership

The Tragedy of the Common To-dos

Daily Standup Day 1: Who's on first?

Developer Terry: "I had a question for PM Val about what it means to 'log user activity'. I'm not sure what activity he means. I haven't heard back yet. I'm starting with page view counts because I think that's what Val would say."

Developer Jan: "I wasn't sure about part of the UX design. In the sense that there isn't one. I wanted to run my modification to this reports page by UX designer Anh. I emailed her last week, but I forgot to email her again this week."

PM Val: "That Epic has been ready for work for two weeks. Did you need something?"

Developer Fran: "Deepu started testing it last week, but then I realized I forgot to do a couple things. I think it's mostly ready for testing again."

M. McCormick, *The Agile Codex*, https://doi.org/10.1007/978-1-4842-7280-0_1

QE Deepu: "I asked Terry about some strange behavior I saw in that Story but didn't hear back. It seemed ok so I just closed it."

PM Val: "I delivered all the User Stories for this Epic two weeks ago. Why haven't they been started?"

Imagine a software project as a pile of shared to-do lists. When the list is created, each stakeholder dutifully fills out what they imagine their personal to-dos on that list should be. The to-dos start and stop and start again. Some complete. Some get paused for a while. To-dos are added and removed and assigned by various individuals over time.

Every to-do owner, if they are the responsible type, also has their own list which represents all their to-dos scattered across all the other lists. They need to keep this list up to date with the priorities and status of each to-do, including whether any given to-do is blocked by an external to-do or must be done before any other to-do in their own list. As to-dos are added and removed and completed and unblocked in the other lists, their reflections in the personal list must get updated as well.

Shared Lists

To the individual, their reality is their own list, and the reflection is in the shared lists. Figure 1-1 depicts this split perspective.

What the Person Thinks

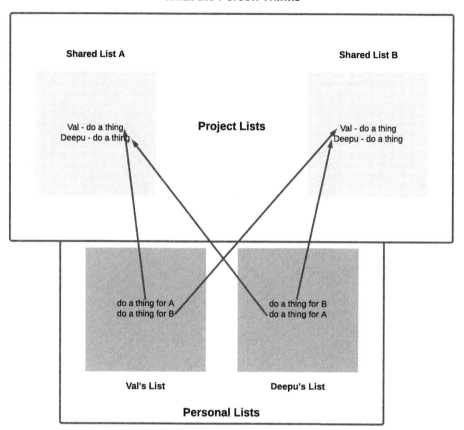

Figure 1-1. Shared to-dos from the personal perspective

To the project, the reality is the shared lists, and the reflection is scattered across all the individual lists. If the shared lists are not complete, the project is not complete. Figure 1-2 shows this reality from the perspective of the project.

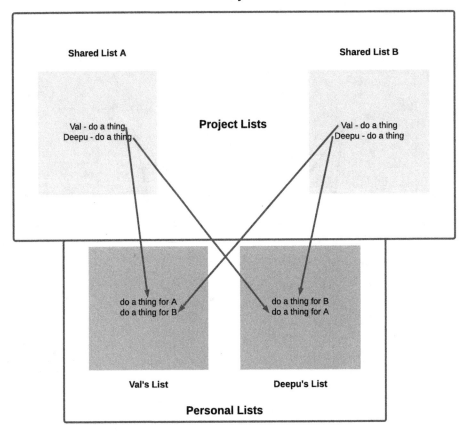

Figure 1-2. Shared to-dos from the project perspective

If you were the blocker, and you just finished your work, you would need to know what you were blocking, who owns it, how to contact them, *and* that you need to tell them you are done. If you were blocked, you would need to have a way to be contacted, a way to know what to-do has gotten unblocked, and where it should go on your personal pile of to-dos. You would also need to tell the blocker that you received their message. If any message is not acknowledged in either direction, the sender needs to know, track, and remember to retry.

The message content itself needs to be unambiguous, as any ambiguity means another round trip, or a shortcut – an assumption about what is *meant* by the message – which may or may not be correct, and which likely will not get communicated back to the sender.

Needless to say, this shared to-do list system is complicated and error prone. It is very easy and indeed likely for the personal lists to get out of sync with the shared lists.

Ownership

The common thread connecting each of these updates is about *ownership*. In each case, someone either

- Believed that they had handed something to another person
- They didn't realize they were supposed to hand something to another person
- They didn't realize they had received something
- Or they made an assumption about what they were handed

In all cases, work stopped, or the wrong work was done.

The shared to-do list is a classic example of the problem of *shared ownership*. Because no one owns the shared list, synchronization errors have no systematic way of being corrected. If there were an owner of the shared list, that owner would be clearly responsible for tracking the state of each to-do and ensuring that they were reflected correctly in the individual lists. The owner would also be responsible for ensuring the integrity of each to-do in the context of the purpose of the list – that is, does each to-do *make sense* to be on the list, and is each to-do clearly fulfilling the reason the list exists?

Absent this shared list owner, teams rely on individuals with outsized senses of responsibility to exercise their consciences and try to coordinate things for the greater good. But these individuals are primarily measured by and incentivized to the fulfillment of their personal lists. While management may laud their extra mile efforts, if anything on the personal list slips as a result, there is rarely forgiveness.

Having only local knowledge, the volunteers are not able to make optimal decisions. They simply do not have enough information. Getting this information is yet another burden and friction on their attempts to do good. They often do not know what information they lack, nor do they know for sure where to get it. They become nags or make assumptions that prove incorrect and disruptive.

These volunteers, as volunteers, also lack explicit authority. Their attempts to inquire and delegate work may be ignored or even rebuffed. Knowing this, their attempts may also be couched in enough polite verbiage to not even resemble an ask at all. Follow-up on ignored requests would so resemble a nag as to only happen in the most extreme situations.

Over time, doing multiple jobs, alone, burns these volunteers out. Being rebuffed or ignored gives the impression that people do not care or share the same commitment to the cause. The volunteers silently withdraw from volunteering, absorbing the culture they perceive and retreating to servicing their personal lists, and viewing their dependencies as threats instead of supporters, and collaboration as cost, not opportunity. Some leave their jobs altogether.

There is a third, more insidious vector of this ambiguity, which is that it opens a psychological door that some are more than happy to unconsciously walk through. Questions and problems can be difficult, nuanced, and take time to think through and answer well. Schedules are full and distractions are everywhere. Pressure is high. By creating a two-way habit of plausible deniability – "I thought you had it. You thought I had it." – the work may remain, but everyone is off the hook.

It is not uncommon for this ambiguity to persist to the point it becomes a cultural norm. I have been in a number of meetings where one leader says to another, when faced with a particularly difficult conundrum to solve, "Let's follow up offline," which serves as an acceptable signal to the group that, yes, it will be solved, and an implicit signal between the leaders that, "I won't bring it up again if you won't..." while silencing the internal guilt with the hope that "in time, it might just solve itself."

Untangling

This shared ownership problem perfectly described the state my new team was in. Recognizing this, the first order of business was to assign owners to the shared lists. Each owner was a member of the development team and a direct report to me. Having a direct reporting line allowed me to also assure them that they had the authority and the responsibility to do the work.

As the owners were all peers, and ownership was distributed evenly among the team, there was no explicit authority I could imbue in them with respect to their peers in terms of an organizational reporting chart. Instead, I vested them with the authority of the *process and accountability*.

By standardizing the process and elevating the process to a first-class citizen, it was clear that any implicit attempts to claim authority by the area owner were in fact intrinsically justified by my blessing of the process itself. They were not doing it to nag or self-aggrandize – they were doing it because it was their job description.

Accountability went both ways, as well, for the process described and demanded it as well. I made it clear to the team that if you are contacted by an owner, you are responsible for responding, and if you contact another owner, they are just as responsible as you to respond. The personal list was no longer the primary measure of performance.

I added an extra layer of accountability by requiring that these communications be recorded in writing. Direct messaging tools and Jira tickets held and archived these public conversations and made it difficult to avoid resolving challenging problems. It became much more difficult to lead conversations into an early death by ambiguity.

These newly deputized owners were tasked first with just taking inventory. I asked them to investigate their lists and their to-dos and either modify or eject any which did not serve the purpose of the list. If they thought of anything which should be on the list but was not, they were to add it. If something got lost in the process, so be it. If it were important, it would resurface as such. Absorbing these losses was far less expensive than continuing to plow forward without any coordinated plan at all.

What we found was that many lists had become dumping grounds of various teams' to-dos. The stated purpose of each list was unclear, and as a result, the criteria for a to-do to belong were subject to interpretation. As to-dos often are, many were themselves vague, making it difficult to know what would even constitute its completion.

Cleanup of these to-dos also included ejecting any to-dos which were outside of engineering's authority to manage or complete. Because we could not know what other teams' priorities were, we had no way of optimizing the completion of our work if other teams could arbitrarily stop us from doing the things we were tasked to do because of their competing workloads or priorities.

While we certainly needed inputs from other teams, and provided output to other teams, we clarified the contents and sequence of these inputs and outputs to be on *either side* of our own to-dos. This vastly simplified our model and allowed us to apply a *life cycle* to the *lifetime* of the list. Each point in the life cycle was the responsibility of the owner of the grouped to-dos before ours, and our to-dos could not be started until those upstream to-dos were complete.

Simply by looking at the current life cycle phase of a list, a team could know if they were needed and that they were blocking it moving forward until they did their work. Once they were complete, the life cycle changed, and the next owner could take over.

In short, we changed our process from an "unphased shared to-dos" model to a "single-owner input / output life cycle" model, as shown in Figure 1-3.

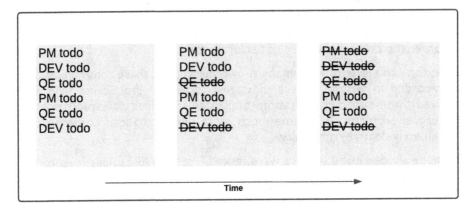

Unphased Shared To-Dos

PM todo	PM todo	~~PM todo~~
DEV todo	DEV todo	~~DEV todo~~
QE todo	~~QE todo~~	~~QE todo~~
PM todo	PM todo	PM todo
QE todo	QE todo	QE todo
DEV todo	~~DEV todo~~	~~DEV todo~~

Time →

Single-Owner Input / Output Life Cycle

PM	DEV	QE
PM todo	~~PM todo~~	~~PM todo~~
PM todo	~~PM todo~~	~~PM todo~~
DEV todo	DEV todo	~~DEV todo~~
DEV todo	DEV todo	~~DEV todo~~
QE todo	QE todo	QE todo
QE todo	QE todo	QE todo

Figure 1-3. From unphased, shared to-dos to single-owner input / output life cycle

As becomes apparent in these diagrams, these lists could easily represent User Stories.

The practical steps we took were to restructure the workflow of the User Stories and to define and arrange the responsibilities toward the User Stories in such a way that they could and should only be executed in the life cycle order: if the User Story is in the PM phase, the PM is responsible for executing the work required to prepare it for transition to the next phase, the DEV is responsible for the work in the DEV phase, and QE for work in the QE phase.

Most of the User Stories in-flight had to be untangled and rebuilt into new User Stories or flagged to retroactively capture the missing tasks from bypassed phases. The untangling exposed the outages and forced us to more clearly and concisely identify the definition of the work within the boundaries of the workflow.

It was both painful and eye-opening to realize how ill-defined the work was and how much debt we were in from a planning perspective. It also revealed an explanation for the reality of why code was being written but no progress was being made.

Small, Independent Units of Work

Scope Matters

Daily Standup Day 2: Merge conflicts!

Developer Terry: "I spent the day resolving merge conflicts."

Developer Jan: "I had all my merge conflicts resolved until Terry checked in."

Developer Fran: "I had all my merge conflicts resolved until Jan and Terry checked their stuff in."

As a best practice, developers do their work by branching off of the main code line for each User Story they work on. On this branch, their changes are isolated from impacting the main branch. Once they have completed their work, they attempt to merge the changes back to the main line. A merge

© Michael McCormick 2021
M. McCormick, *The Agile Codex*, https://doi.org/10.1007/978-1-4842-7280-0_2

conflict occurs when their changes conflict with changes that occurred to the same area of code during the time between the creation of their feature branch and completion of their work.

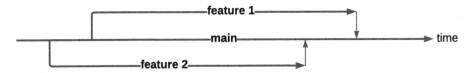

Figure 2-1. Simultaneous feature branch life cycle

There are three principal vectors which influence the likelihood of a merge conflict:

- The breadth of the codebase being touched:

  The more code you are changing, the more likely you will collide with another set of changes.

- The amount of time the feature branch is open:

  The longer you wait to merge, the more time there is for other developers to make changes that might be in the same area of code.

- The amount of concurrent work happening in an area of code:

  If multiple people are changing a given piece of functionality at the same time, the more likely it is their changes will collide.

The common denominator in all three is the *scope* of work being done on the feature branch. When a User Story involves work that touches a lot of code, or work that takes a lot of time, its scope is considered large. The larger the scope, the more likely it is, statistically speaking, to also encompass areas of functionality being worked on by others.

Resolving merge conflicts can be expensive. They are, by definition, not machine resolvable. This means that the logic or semantics of the change conflict with others. When logic or semantic changes need to be resolved, there is a risk that the intent of the code in the main branch could be unintentionally modified, causing unexpected behavior and bugs. It takes time, and sometimes conversations, for a developer to be absolutely sure their resolution preserves the original intent.

Sometimes the changes logically contradict, requiring a revisiting of the feature intent of all the involved work, a new design, new User Stories, and a refreshed feature branch or two to put it all together again. New designs, new User Stories, and revisiting feature intents involve product managers, new tests, doc updates, and possibly even new UX designs.

Having a long-lived feature branch is not always desired, at least by the developer doing the work. There is overhead to every feature branch merge that goes beyond merge conflicts: there are code reviews, associated User Stories to update, designs to refresh, and testing to support, to name a few. When a lot of changes need to happen, it can be optimal, from the individual's perspective, to do them all at once, so as to batch all those touchpoints into one. In a culture where developers just throw work over the wall to QE, this is without question an incentivized path. Why worry about risky check-ins when the cost is borne by another team?

This incentive is also strong when a developer does not actually know *how* the implementation will be done, or even *what* the implementation will consist of. In this approach, one makes a lot of sweeping changes, experiments, backs up, and repeats. If each experiment were checked in, there would be more work and explanation and overhead to back up and try another one.

It is a hard and fast truth about software development that these experiments need to happen. In fact, they are the core of innovation. And they certainly should not be disincentivized. Once the experimenting is done, and the design and implementation are proven, it is then up to the developer to construct the implementation plan as a set of properly structured, individual, small-scoped User Stories.

This experimental branch is never checked in. Instead, as each of the new, smaller User Stories is branched onto their own sequential feature branches, implemented, and merged, conflicts are contained and any contradictions in the implementation plan with existing code are immediately surfaced.

There is one other reason a developer might hold a feature branch open for a long time: lack of planning. When tools and processes devalue or otherwise do not support or encourage planning, it is not difficult to slide down the slippery slope and to begin treating *everything* as an experiment by default.

Clearly, there is great benefit to reducing the scope of a given User Story, to ensure the life of the feature branch is short, the amount of code involved is small, and the work covers a narrower part of any feature area. There is less harm in having a sequence of small User Stories to encompass a larger change than there is in dealing with significant or risky merge conflicts. More importantly, as in many aspects of life, taking some short-term pain to plan, no matter how counterintuitive it may feel to the impatient, will pay off handsomely in the death by a thousand cuts of short-term thinking.

Daily Standup Day 3: Need a reviewer!

Developer Lee: "I have been waiting three days for a code review. My feature branch is getting out of date. Can someone please look at it?"

Developer Fran: "Sorry Lee. It is taking me a long time to get through the review because of how many things you are changing."

A typical development flow involves submitting the feature branch for review by other developers before merging it to the main branch. When a developer feels that the code is ready for merge, other developers can review, comment, approve, or reject the work. Once all the required reviewers have approved, the work can then be merged into the main branch.

This review process services a couple of key purposes. First, it ensures code quality and consistency, as reviewers are generally individuals who understand the feature and code environment well enough to spot deviations from architectural intent as well as to identify errors and sloppy logic. The second purpose is to provide a means of communication – as new code enters the system, the presence, shape, and purpose of the code is socialized with the reviewers as part of the review process itself.

As such, reviews must be structured in such a way as to be maximally efficient in terms of clarity of what is being reviewed. Review comments should also be quick and efficient to respond to, so the response can be parsed and verified just as quickly. Efficiency of this sort requires the scope of any change to be small and safe.

So again, we face the problem of scope. The larger the scope of work, the more risk there is. The more risk there is, the more care must be taken in reviewing a change before approving it to be merged back to the main branch. Sweeping architectural changes, implicit or explicit, are more likely to occur, the greater the scope, as well as unintended side effects.

Changes which need to be made in response to review also take longer, as more moving parts are involved, and more logical code paths need to be thought through for regression risk and architectural integrity.

Reviews are also interruptions for other developers who are busy writing their own code. The deeper and more complex a review needs to be, the more concentration is required, the larger the context switch, and therefore the larger the block of time which needs to be allocated to be free of interruptions. This disincentives developers from volunteering to do reviews, and those most qualified to do the reviews also tend to have the most responsibility around delivering their own code.

Reducing the scope of the work allows for much less expensive context switching, much simpler reviews, and quicker and safer changes as a result of the reviews. The reviewers, able as a result to be more productive in delivering their own code, are more incentivized to be responsive to requests for review.

Daily Standup Day 4: I broke some stuff. I think.

Developer Fran: "I made some changes to all of the search engine algorithms and after merging it back, the main branch is behaving a little differently than it was in my feature branch."

QE Deepu: "Fran, it looks like all the car image searches are now returning cat .gifs!"

Developer Terry: "It might also be my changes that I merged right after you."

Developer Jan: "Or mine, that I merged right before you."

Developer Lee: "I have a change to one of the algorithms I need to make but I'm holding off now until we get this resolved."

While changes which reach deep into shared utility code can cause unanticipated side effects, it is not often difficult to track the blast radius as it funnels upward through the API layer.

It is far riskier in most cases to make changes across a broad swath of application logic where interactions between modules take functional precedence. These areas of code can cover much of the application behavior like a blanket where small changes can influence application behavior in unintended ways. As Figure 2-2 shows, this blast radius is flatter and more complex to untangle. Like multiple interacting medicines with side effects of their own, the more of these changes made at once, the more complex the diagnosis and the more fraught the untangling.

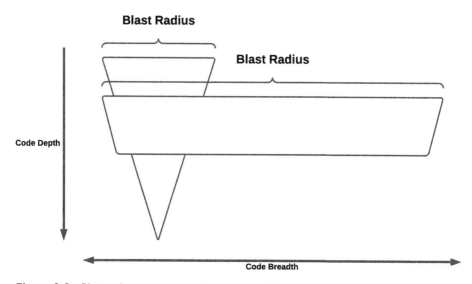

Figure 2-2. Blast radius comparison: deep versus wide

Finding and remediating the regressions from changes like these can take a long time. Changes happening around them can further cloud the scene. These train wrecks can shut down the tracks for days as the wreckage is cleared.

By keeping the scope of work small, the blast radius can be limited even when the shape is less predictable. If not entirely avoided, complex regressions can be much simpler to remediate when the changes in question are small and quick to appear and just as quick to revert or trace for the root cause.

As the scope of the work increases, the cost to close increases exponentially (see Figure 2-3).

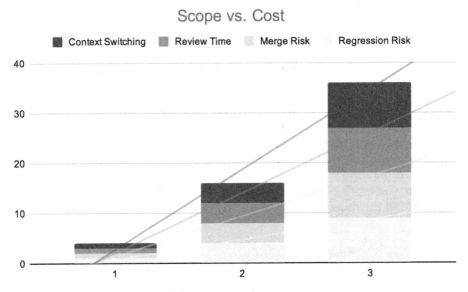

Figure 2-3. Cost to close as scope of work increases

Daily Standup Day 5: Turns out I need this other thing.

Developer Lee: "I was making a change across the User API. They were simple, low-risk, optional parameter additions across all sixteen endpoints. After I got halfway done, I realized I also need to implement obfuscation algorithms since we may be carrying and persisting new personally identifiable information. Not only will that take twice as long, I need to wait for Terry to implement the encryption utility that's not scheduled until next month as part of the PII logging library User Story."

Developer Terry: "I'll do the obfuscation algorithm task, but I don't want to bring the User Story out of the backlog since I won't be actually working on it for a while yet. I can't do the logging refactoring task of my User Story for the User API until you finish the API updates."

Broad changes, even when superficially simple, can carry a multiplicative effect on workload when new scope is discovered during implementation. Sixteen copy and paste changes across an API plane can quickly morph into sixteen custom implementations of code underneath, introducing more risk and requiring much more time to resolve.

These types of changes also carry with them a greater risk that unseen dependencies for small pieces of the work will appear, simply because the bigger the change, the more dependencies there are. When these dependencies also live as smaller parts of other User Stories, a circular dependency arises.

The most expedient and common way this is addressed is by working tasks independently of the life cycle of the User Story. When this happens, the ownership becomes disconnected from the way the state of the User Story is represented, sending incorrect signals about who is to do what and when.

In the example diagram, Lee expected to add a parameter and obfuscate the PII. After getting started, Lee realized that the PII could not be obfuscated yet because the obfuscation utility had not yet been written. That work is still in the Backlog and has not yet even been groomed and made ready for work. Having no grooming, QE does not know how it will work or how to test it. Operations does not know how the obfuscation utility itself may need to be deployed or managed from a security auditing standpoint.

As Terry volunteers to get that piece done to unblock Lee, all of those quality gates are skipped. The PM, QE, and Operations teams have no workflow trigger to know that the work is being done without grooming, decisions will be made without their input, and work will either bypass them altogether, or arrive on their doorstep without warning or adequate preparation. Every time this happens, individuals are relied upon to shepherd work through the bypass of flow, and this reliance on individuals taking on extra vigilance and care is a recipe for accidents down the line. Errors are likely, memories will fail in time, and accidents will happen. Figure 2-4 depicts Terry and Lee's predicament.

What Terry and Lee Planned To Do

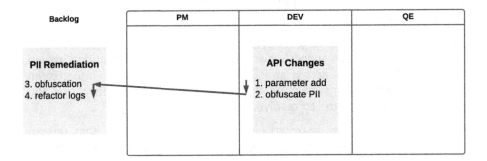

What Terry and Lee Actually Have To Do

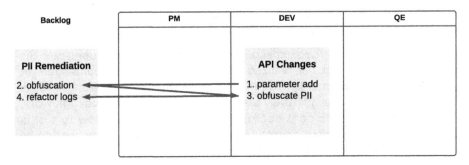

Figure 2-4. A broken life cycle caused by out of order dependencies

Keeping the scope of work small prevents risk of exploding effort time, calendar delays due to dependencies, and User Stories being forced out of their life cycle due to cyclic dependencies across User Stories. In fact, one of the most reliable system signals for this situation is when a User Story lingers on the Board for a long time. Any time the calendar time starts expanding long past effort time, there is often an untracked dependency in the way.

On our team, as each User Story owner redefined the work to align to the life cycle, we were forced to not only keep the tasks isolated as dependencies, but we also found that the smaller the scope of the User Story, the fewer tasks it needed, and the easier it was to achieve that isolation.

As our User Stories were cleaned up and conformed to the life cycle, they shrank as well and began flowing through the life cycle more efficiently. Shorter feature branches, fewer merge conflicts, simple quick reviews, safer changes meant less time spent off of the main branch, simpler merges, more willing and available reviewers, and fewer regressions. Finally, when unexpected scope or dependencies arose, they were efficiently resolvable without breaking the User Story life cycles.

More importantly, the process of learning to think of the User Stories as small, and the tasks as encapsulated and isolated to the User Stories, starts to build an important muscle in the team – an ability to think deeply enough about the work that that detailed planning became something more than a theoretical nice-to-have – it became both possible and worth doing.

Sized

How Much and How Long?

Daily Standup Day 6: Five hours or five weeks…

Developer Terry: "I might be done tomorrow but maybe it will be next week."

When I arrived, few of the User Stories had points assigned. Which is not surprising, given their hollow levels of description and cursory degrees of consideration. By not having sizes on the User Stories, it was impossible to make any predictions of when any given User Story would be delivered.

Under enormous amounts of pressure, the team had quickly generated User Stories as anything from ad hoc to-do lists to simplified placeholders for internal intuitions and plans about what work they signified. What had begun by necessity became the cultural norm; by removing the pressure to size a User Story, there was no longer a need to define or plan a User Story to that level of detail.

Nor was there any guidepost for when a User Story should reasonably be delivered. While some may rail against the undue pressure that a sized User Story can put on a developer when circumstances have expanded the scope of work, there is a far more reasonable effect of pointing a User Story: When a User Story becomes more or less work than originally anticipated, the

M. McCormick, *The Agile Codex*, https://doi.org/10.1007/978-1-4842-7280-0_3

change in sizing becomes a *measurable signal*. In the short term, this signal can be used to update completion projections and dependencies. In the long term, patterns of scope changes can indicate opportunities for systemic improvement in planning and execution.

By planning a User Story to the level of detail that it could be sized, one is also able to express that detail in writing and, by doing that, make the User Story a transferable and durable source of truth for the work to be done. Without this drive to detail, designs, if they exist at all, are more likely to remain in one developer's mind. The work done to implement the User Story leaves only its literal trace in code and memory, inaccessible to those who do not have time or skill to dig through weeks or months of code changes or to interrupt the developer with a fraught memory exercise.

Lastly, the relative size of Epics could not be compared with any reliable resolution, as their constituent User Stories were not sized and could not be summed. Without being able to understand the true scope of work in an Epic, it was impossible to prioritize Epics relative to each other. For example, if one Epic might take half the time remaining in the release, it may make sense to reduce its scope or remove it in favor of others.

The most insidious effect of the inability to plan is the resulting cultural inertia and learned helplessness toward planning at all. Inability becomes unwillingness. On this team, the emergency behavior became the default behavior, with the implication that planning was simply not something that was done or expected. Most developers are courteous and conscientious to a fault. A culture which pushes against those traits of character, frustrating the best intentions, demotivates the strongest performers and attracts their opposite.

Thus began the iterative process of sizing our User Stories. As the owners cleaned and organized them into small, independent units of work with clear and accurate descriptions and designs, the ability to scope that work in terms of effort time became simple.

Once the User Stories were defined and sized in this way, we also gained the flexibility to have any developer work on any User Story without having to make assumptions, read minds, or interrupt people to explain to them what they were supposed to do.

Because properly sizing a User Story requires an adequate definition of what needs to be done and how it will be done, UX and technical designs as well as product and technical requirements became the medium for delivering that plan in a common language.

Some of the Epics which had been sized so optimistically were corrected and grew significantly. The developers who had been feeling pressured to under-size the Epics now had data and evidence to answer the question: "It's so simple. How can it take a month to do *that?*" and were thus empowered to push back with a dose of cold reality.

This level of data and justifiability went the other way as well. Senior leadership began to regain trust in the development team and their commitments, as they witnessed a level of understanding of the work that raised intelligent questions and made room for nuanced answers.

Trust was further enhanced as progress toward completion became measurable and more predictable, and unexpected changes could be analyzed, explained, and remediated with continued learning.

Developers gained more evidence in not only the value of planning and thinking deeply about the work, but also in their ability to do this planning and thinking. They were also able to see and measure their own progress and get signaled more reliably about their dependencies' delivery dates. They could shuffle work between each other based on skill and expediency. Interruptions declined and self-sufficiency grew. People started speaking the same language about the design and with it, their understanding of the product and architectural intent became both motivating and habitual.

The virtuous cycle grew, and the culture started to change. The conscientious were rewarded with a framework that encouraged conscientiousness and their examples began to change the norm, and with it, the entire team.

Sequenced

When?

___

Daily Standup Day 7: ...or five hours over five weeks?

Developer Jan: "I'm halfway done with the API change, a third of the way done with the login page, and just about finished with the registration page."

Developer Lee: "I am waiting on Jan's login page before I can do the reset password page. So, in the meantime I'm working on the logging API and the location search algorithms."

Developer Terry: "I am waiting on the logging API work before I do the page navigation implementation, so I'm not sure what to do next. I'll probably pick up a couple more User Stories."

In its pure form during planning, User Story sizing indicates one thing: how much developer time needs to be spent to complete the User Story. The purpose of this from the perspective of planning is twofold:

- Manage allocation of available developer time to work that needs to be done:

M. McCormick, *The Agile Codex*, https://doi.org/10.1007/978-1-4842-7280-0_4

Developers only have a certain number of hours in a day that they can be executing on a User Story. Sizing is key to managing their workload and ensuring that the amount of work they take on can be finished in the time allotted.

- Predict when work will be done:

  The sum total of work compared with the sum total of available resources allows a project planner to scope a project within reasonable guidelines and make commitments with varying degrees of accuracy. Well-estimated User Stories are important inputs around providing this accuracy and justifying commitments.

There is a nuance to the second point, which is critical to explore, and that is around what it means to say "work." All work? Some work? All work across all developers? One piece of work for one developer?

The longer the scope and broader the measure across the team, the more obvious the calculus. There are no intervening variables. We simply say "given no risk or changes, all the work costs X and all the resources are available to give Y / day so we will deliver in X / (Y * number of developers) days" (Figure 4-1).

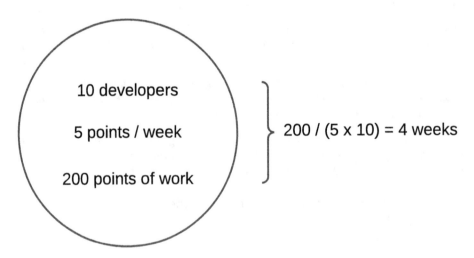

10 developers

5 points / week

200 points of work

200 / (5 x 10) = 4 weeks

Figure 4-1. Time to complete with full parallelization of work

When we look at a smaller resolution, we start to see gaps in this idealistic view. If we define work as one User Story, we will say that a 5-point User Story started on Monday would be completed on Friday.

Even assuming that these 5 points of velocity account for the general overhead and interrupts of the day, how many teams would actually see this happen in real life? Nearly zero. Why? Because a developer rarely works on only one User Story at a time.

The principal reason a developer would pause one User Story to pick up another User Story is the paused User Story is waiting on a *dependency*. There is something that it needs that is not yet done. So, the developer starts another User Story. Then that one gets blocked, and they start another. Eventually one gets unblocked, so they jump back and finish it off.

Developer Lee's 5-point User Story that would be finished on Friday is still not finished on the following Friday. But one other User Story got done and another is partly done.

Imagine Jan is depending on Lee to deliver a User Story. How will Jan know when Lee's dependency will be delivered? It wasn't last Friday and now it's not this Friday either. Now what happens when Lee is waiting on Terry who also is delivering in this choppy manner?

In a world where context switching is free, we can still say in all this jumble that all the User Stories will be delivered when we predicted at the beginning. What we cannot do is reliably predict when a given User Story will arrive. Figure 4-2 depicts this flow in a Gantt form.

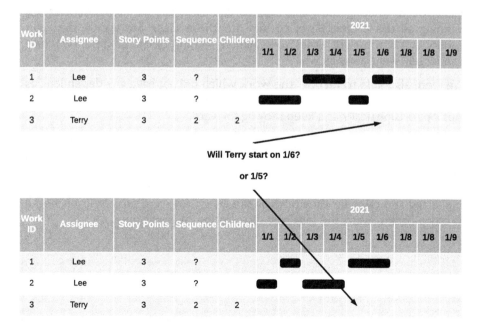

Figure 4-2. Unpredictable delivery times cause unpredictable start times

Approaching the work in this manner, developers quickly get into a state where they are *blocked*. They simply have no work they can reasonably do while they wait. They could even become permanently gridlocked if a cyclic dependency surfaced.

These gaps, these waiting times, cause the *calendar* time of a delivery to grow beyond the sum total of *effort* time. If there are 200 points of work, and 10 developers worked on 5 points a week without any gaps, we saw it was 4 *calendar* weeks to deliver. Effort weeks equals calendar weeks. If all 10 developers, over the course of the release, had to wait a cumulative week for dependencies to unblock them, the amount of effort is still 200 points, but the amount of time is now 5 calendar weeks.

Context-switching is most definitely not free and is in fact incredibly deleterious to developer productivity. Environments and builds may need to be switched and reconstructed when changing feature branches. The train of thought that was driving the work before it was put down needs to be entirely reconstructed. The lifetime of the feature branch has been extended, risking merge conflicts, lengthy reviews and quality regressions. In effect, context switching between small pieces of work negates all the benefit gained from creating the work as small and independent units in the first place.

As my team took ownership and repaired the User Stories, it became clear which other User Stories they depended on. We were then able to identify which User Stories should happen in which order so as to minimize the likelihood of waiting time and also to eliminate circular dependencies. By planning at the project level to allocate these User Stories to the right developers at the right times to minimize waiting times, context switching pain largely went away as well.

We were also able to identify the work which did *not* have any dependencies at all. When gaps did appear, it was a simple matter to pull this work into the gaps opportunistically and keep moving forward.

As before, the muscle of planning continued to grow. The deep thinking that went into this kind of User Story construction continued to pay off. Developers were able to focus on executing one User Story at a time, and they learned to identify the sequence of work that made the most sense. Gaps were minimized and calendar time both at the User Story and project levels began to creep back toward the idealistic distribution of effort time.

Inputs, Transition Criteria, Outputs

Setting Boundaries

Daily Standup Day 8: Did you say something?

Developer Jan: "After starting my new User Story last week, I realized I'm not sure what PM Val meant by 'User Activity Logging' in the description so I'm on hold until I can get clarification."

QE Deepu: "I just got Jan's User Story for testing and I can't tell what I'm supposed to test. I could be wrong, but it doesn't seem fully implemented."

PM Val: "Jan, I didn't realize you needed anything."

© Michael McCormick 2021
M. McCormick, *The Agile Codex*, https://doi.org/10.1007/978-1-4842-7280-0_5

In Chapter 1, "Clear Ownership," I introduced the concept of the Single Owner Input / Output Life Cycle, wherein as the User Story moves through each life cycle phase, a single person is responsible for executing their set of the ordered, segregated list of tasks.

Without this life cycle segregation, there is no clear and reliable *systemic* signal around what is needed, who needs to give it and by when, why it is needed, or what is to be done with it once it is received. Instead, we end up back in the shared list paradigm, where we rely on individuals to be aware of non-local effects of local optimizations – something they cannot be relied upon to have the information to do effectively.

In addition to organizing the work in order of the life cycle phase's owner, we also need rules around how the phase is *changed*. The change of phase is triggered when the owner of the phase completes required tasks to prepare the work for the next phase and transfer to the next owner. To do this, there needs to be a clear understanding of who the current owner is, what inputs are required and from whom they come, how the inputs are assessed in order to validate the transition, and a common definition and format for the outputs of the work (Figure 5-1).

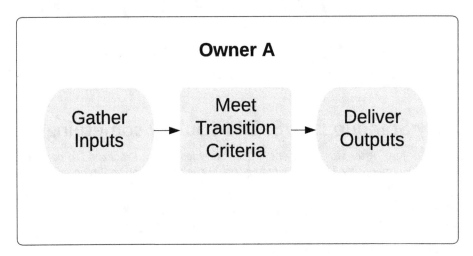

Figure 5-1. The phase life cycle

It is the role of the owner to drive transition of the work to the next phase: to gather the inputs, assess and validate the transition criteria, and document the outputs.

The system can then enforce guardrails by clearly signaling to the individual when work has transitioned to their ownership, by enforcing documentation of the transition reasoning and operations, and by not allowing the work to transition phases until the output conforms to specification.

As we went through the process of reconstructing our User Stories, we had to align their current state with the life cycle phase they belonged in, as many User Stories were already in progress and out of compliance with the phase change rules we had established.

To remediate, we created special labels and color codes for the board to indicate the retroactive work needed, such as "Need UX" in the case where designs were not complete before work started, and "Need PM" for situations where the full requirements were unclear when work started. We did not make a special column on the board to indicate these disconnects, as they do not represent phases and therefore would overload the visual meaning of columns as phases and phases only.

We also established rules around how long an owner would wait for information before being empowered to make a unilateral decision. This allowed us to continue moving forward while at the same time emphasizing to our dependencies the need to be responsive and involved. All decisions, unilateral or not, were documented in the User Story.

These labels and colors became very useful flags to help us identify when the transition criteria and outputs were ambiguously defined, causing User Stories to prematurely escape their upstream phases. We were able to quickly iterate on these outages to the point at which leakage became both rare and minor.

Even in a smoothly running machine there will be times where we do not think of everything in advance or we discover things along the way which need clarification or interjection from an upstream dependency, such as a design that does not quite work as expected or a requirement for an edge case no one thought of. This same process helps us not only remediate the outages, it also helps us identify the kinds of outages we have, giving us valuable information and practice to close those gaps with new understandings, so they become less likely to occur. We learn the *kinds* of questions to ask and the areas where we need to take extra time to think through before beginning work.

This process of refinement continues on every project I own, as every project differs in organization, personnel, skills, type of work, length of project, level of planning required, and so on. Each difference exposes an opportunity to refine the contracts and practice anew.

Stakeholder Approval

Succeed As a Team

Daily Standup Day 9: Oops. I forgot to tell you. Or ask you.

Developer Terry: "This User Story I was just assigned for this Sprint is missing some acceptance criteria. PM Val, can we meet after this to go over them?"

QE Deepu: "I just got Lee's User Story for testing and this is going to require a lot of work to set up a new test harness. I wish I had known beforehand. The testing on this is going to be late."

Developer Lee: "Where are the UX designs for this User Story I just started, UX designer Anh?"

A machine system, on its own, can only partially enforce life cycle contracts of owner, inputs, transition criteria, and outputs. The objects which move

M. McCormick, *The Agile Codex*, https://doi.org/10.1007/978-1-4842-7280-0_6

through phases (Epics and User Stories, in the Agile world) are the domain of natural language. While language can be contained in them, only the presence or absence of it can be reliably judged by the machine.

While the owner can be the most conscientious judge of whether or not the inputs are adequate, the transition criteria have been met, and outputs conform, the owner still suffers from the problem of *locality*.

The owner cannot know what information is needed for the context of the project, and most specifically, the downstream owners of the work. The owner also lacks the domain knowledge and judgment that the other roles are specialized to provide.

As such, the process of gathering inputs, assessing transition criteria, and approving outputs must involve every stakeholder in the work. The owner retains the responsibility to guide and moderate the process, and drive to the transition approval. The group is responsible for participating by providing the needed inputs, assessing the acceptability of the criteria from their context, and approving the outputs and subsequent phase transition via sign-off.

This democratic process of stakeholder approval became the key to team cohesion. By grooming the work together, every stakeholder on our team took on the responsibility to ensure that when the work transitioned to them, it would contain the information needed for them to do their part:

- QE asked all the questions around edge cases and design for testability.

- The documentation writer made sure the designs and acceptance criteria did not conflict, to ensure they could correctly communicate the product functionality to the customer.

- The developer and PM iteratively refined product acceptance criteria in order to be clearly translatable to technical acceptance criteria.

- The operations engineer raised issues and advised on conformance to deployment pipelines and operational access.

- The UX designer provided context for discussions around look and feel, usability, and information architecture, all of which led to group explorations around edge cases, customer experience, and API requirements to support the designs.

Through repetition of these conversations, the grooming teams quickly created a shared language to talk about the inputs and criteria, and each one built a mental template of the pieces of the puzzle they needed to provide and push against to suit their concerns and expertise.

Figure 6-1 depicts the grooming and sign-off of a User Story in this model, where the developer owns the phase, the participants provide input, and then those same participants provide sign-off. In our Agile flow, the completion of these steps triggered a phase change for the User Story from "Needs Sign-Off" to "Signed-Off, Ready for Work."

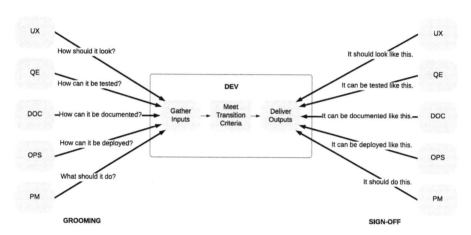

Figure 6-1. Phase transition from "Needs Sign-Off" to "Signed Off, Ready for Work"

This culture of accountability and cooperation, and this shared language, became the most critical tool in improving our productivity. Quality of life and enjoyment of work went up. Relationships grew and strengthened between the team members. Trust became abundant.[1] With everyone rowing in the same direction, the boat became swift, and steerable.

Oh, and we shipped on time. Barely.

---

[1] One developer said, right near the end: "It's funny. We're under the most pressure we've ever felt, and we still *like* each other."

The Agile Codex Theory

Prologue

Every assumption is a dependency. Every dependency is a risk.

From forest to sawmill, wheat field to granary, from warehouse to factory, factory to home, the question is always the same:

"When will it be delivered?"

This question has pursued humankind since the first plant was gathered and the first hunt yielded prey.

Everything we build, we first build in reverse. Applying human intention to the world of cause and effect, we put one and one together. Our human minds, evolved to imagine the future, deconstruct those fantasies into pieces – a set of parts, assembled in a sequence of steps back to the present.

Then, with tools in hand, we turn everything forward again and make it real, one step at a time.

We acknowledge and celebrate the bounty of human variation. Some love to run and hunt. Others are deft with needle and thread. Still others explore the mysteries of taste and texture, sustenance and healing.

We share our labors. The hunter hands the pelt to the tailor, and the meat moves to the butcher and then the cook.

Our imaginations parallelize and allocate. Our practices repeat, evolve, and optimize. In a circle of virtue, social bonds grow, protect, and are protected. Ritual emerges, feeding those bonds, keeping the engines of invention warm through the darkest nights.

Diversity of skill and division of labor support a growing population, in turn feeding the reservoir of productive and inventive possibility. Constructs become more capable. Complexity and interdependence grow.

Sophisticated supply chains form to serve the interdependent makers. The question "When will it be delivered?" becomes a chorus of a thousand voices, each directed to the one before, lighting up the supply lines like neurons in the brain.

While the master teaches the apprentice by doing, the master also hones the telling. When the scribe shares the telling, the recipe becomes the norm. The norms follow the supply lines and become both truth and expectation:

"This is what you are going to get."

As supply lines pump the lifeblood of production, their preservation, efficiency, and flexibility grow. Trade routes form. New forms of transport and packaging make it safer and easier to preserve and move more.

All the while, the circle of invention turns relentlessly inward, building tools to expand the efficiency and ease and possibilities of what can be made. The supply line is a tool. The recipe is a tool. Tools build tools.

With the printing press, information takes a physical, replicable form. Now the recipe is everywhere.

The recipe codifies the expectation:

"This is what you are going to get. Every time."

Make a thing once and you are left with idle tools. Make it twice and your tools are paid for. Make it a thousand times and you are the Industrial Revolution.

The Industrial Age encapsulates the supply line within the factory walls, geared to assembly. With each stage of product conveying past a purpose-built tool, physical workflow is actualized at scale.

"When will it be delivered?" is answered with the clockwork tick of the assembly line.

Assembly lines repurpose, spitting paper. A white-collar workflow is born. Paper shuffles from one specialist to the next, putting the transformation to page and moving to the next specialist in line.

On the factory floor and in the cubicle farm, any surprise – anything that does not fit the pattern – is expensive. When the line stops, it bleeds. Discussions are held. Decisions are escalated. Problems are solved. The solution is systematized and the heart restarts, another step evolved.

An educational system rises to serve these ends. We memorize facts, blank slates run through a rigid school factory, installed to our places as cogs in the Great Machine. Blue collar, white collar, sentenced to life for a pension and the chance to touch the spoils of the Great Expansion.

Industrial engineers and MBAs take root in the factory and office soil – Designers of Assembly and Smokejumpers, imagining backward, tooling forward, on call to capture the spot fires and dig the perimeters, optimizing every flow for speed.

Another revolution. Paper tears into bits and bytes, infinitely replicable, each copy free. The White-Collar River splits into a thousand digitized tributaries and creates the Lake and then Ocean.

Cast free of the chains of physical production, information factories arise. No longer actualizing sameness at scale, production is now the domain of the information artists and architects. Static assembly flows give way to dynamic reconstruction, each widget an answer to the question:

"Is this really what we want?"

The Problem

Doing Is Planning Is Doing Is...

There are inherent tensions in software development. Many of these tensions are often misunderstood as unresolvable contradictions. Every development process theory is an attempt to unravel these tensions, balance them, or remove them altogether. Every development process practice exposes the difficulty in doing so in whichever particular area it breaks down, or needs special care and attention.

There is the tension around how we write down what we are doing when we often do not know for sure what we are doing, and what we do at the beginning is often much different from what we have done in the end.

There is also the tension of how we measure what we do when much of what we do is art.

Another important tension is around how we measure our value as software developers – is it how much code we deliver, or is it how our deliveries of code affect the deliveries of those around us?

Each tension can be boiled down to the trade-off between planning and doing. Either one is thinking about what to do, or one is doing it. For a single person, this trade-off is obvious – the information is all in one brain, as is the history. For a team, choosing how to approach this problem is exponentially complex.

© Michael McCormick 2021
M. McCormick, *The Agile Codex*, https://doi.org/10.1007/978-1-4842-7280-0_7

Plan for the Imperfect Plan

There is never a perfect plan because there is never perfect information. This lack of information generates risk. Information about facts that exist today can be gathered through research or action, and information about what the future may bring comes by just waiting for the future to arrive.

Each software development process theory proscribes an answer, implicitly or explicitly, such as taking measured steps by creating and scheduling research spikes, prototyping or steel threading, or taking slow steps by careful long-term research and group planning, or by just charging ahead to see what shakes out (fail-fast to the extreme). There is rarely a single answer to be settled-on or a single approach to be used. A little bit of all of these can apply at different times.

The process of evaluating progress and approach, embodied in the many rituals of Agile, can also vary between flavors and conditions. How much time is spent measuring and evaluating, and how analyses and recommendations are actioned, can have a large impact on the balance of planning and execution.

Measuring what is happening by turning human inputs and state transitions into data depends on human factors and life cycle architectures which are necessarily imperfect maps on the territory they try to describe. When a nuance occurs that the system is not designed to measure or account for, but has real impact on the overall goal of quality, predictability, and throughput, the system fails to send the correct signal and corrective actions are either not taken, or worse, incorrect actions occur.

What we are *supposed* to do is never exactly what we do, because the situations we encounter evolve and rules that make sense one day make less sense the next. So, we hold our breaths, maybe we make a note, and then we move forward.

Agile processes understand the role of the human when it comes to resolving nuance, adapting the map to the territory as a kind of workflow state buffer (e.g., "I'll remember to do this thing even though it's not explicitly required at this point") or acting to normalize the qualitative judgments (e.g., "After discussion, we all agreed to story point this work at 5"). These processes give room for this kind of activity, and some even adapt the rules, normalizing them to remove them from the list of exceptions.

This process never ends, and risks exploding into complexity, because there will always be exceptions. The norms you expect are the norms you design and plan for. Every project, team, organization, and product are different, and there is no rule book large enough to tell a person what to do in every situation on the ground.

Finding the most efficient way to optimize the process to adapt, capture nuance, emit proper data, and get the best out of each human along the way, is the holy grail of Agile.

Optimize for Adaptability

When we talk about optimizing for adaptability, what we are really talking about is optimizing the map to the territory: How well do we plan, and then reflect the plan and its execution? And when we say "we," about whom do we speak? Planning and execution happen at multiple levels, rolling up near-term focused deliverables into broader visions. Expectations must be set at every level, with details meaningful and available at every resolution.

The bulk of Agile processes idealize the User Story and its Acceptance Criteria and set that as the atomic outcome of the planning and truth of the development workflow. Depending on the projects, the teams, and their organization, a thousand different planning processes and workflows arise, each having a material impact on the nature, construction, and maintenance of the User Story.

Optimizing for adaptability means that any flow of User Stories from planning to execution must be efficiently modifiable. Replanning, which is the organic nature of Agile, must be cheap and quick, and impacts at all levels should be immediately clear through the extent of the release life cycle.

■ **Note** Replanning must be cheap and quick, and impacts at all levels should be immediately clear through the extent of the release life cycle.

Most Agile approaches optimize around three vectors:

- The development of clear requirements: Optimizing for clear requirements means spending time planning before doing work.

- Minimize planning: The typical approach around optimizing for flexibility is to plan just-in-time, and to work just-in-time in parallel with those lightweight plans.

- Total lifetime of the User Story: Reducing the amount of time that a User Story lives reduces the likelihood that it will carry or introduce incidental complexity during its execution and allows the work to become visible more quickly.

The structure of User Stories and the flow through the Agile life cycle change depending on the way these are balanced.

Don't Surrender to Dependencies

With the admirable goal of clear requirements, minimal planning, and short life spans, one large piece falls off the table — dependency tracking. Dependencies are anathema to short life cycles. They introduce calendar time delays to effort time estimates. They affect ordering of work. They require awareness of who is going to work on them so nothing has to wait for a person to free up.

A common theme of Agile, sometimes stated, almost always implied, is that dependencies are hard. This is such a foundational belief that most approaches believe that dealing with dependencies is in contradiction to being Agile at all.

In fact, the very nature of a typical Agile planning process is to pull stories into existence only just before they are needed, thereby avoiding any sort of need to tangle in long-term dependency planning and mapping: We will cross that bridge when we come to it, and in order to be Agile, we will not even assume that it will be a bridge at that point or that we will even have reached it. We will measure and course-correct ten feet, one User Story, or two weeks at a time.

The assumption is that dependencies are an unwinnable war, and no process can possibly do them well without overburdening teams with heavy-handed tracking and eternal planning cycles which risk being thrown away at the first strong breeze during execution.

One typical compromise with the dependency puzzle includes moving toward larger User Stories that encompass all the dependencies in one piece of work, resulting in large, high-risk, high-touch deliveries of code which by their nature risk quality and require stringent reviews. They also reside in long-lived feature branches which can rapidly drift from the main code base.

Large units of work tend to also have higher errors in estimation, especially as they allow for more ambiguity in their definition. Acceptance criteria and test plans can quickly reach a practical combinatorial limit in their expression.

Another approach is to remove cross-functional dependencies by bringing all your dependencies under one roof, one scrum, and even further, to have every resource, every engineer, completely fungible and able to work full-stack on every work item. While this does help to eliminate cross-functional and cross-team dependencies, and strives to eliminate the question of how to schedule the best engineer for the best work item at the best time, it still does not address the simple truth that some things just have to be built in a certain order. And by increasing breadth, one necessarily decreases specialization, a compromise in efficient execution that is felt across the board. Dependencies would need to be incredibly expensive to make that cost worthwhile.

The few Agile forms which accept the reality of dependencies keep User Stories small and manage order of execution by way of backlog ranking. Because backlog is a list and not a tree, it is not simple to arrange the backlog to surface the correct dependencies in the correct order based on who is assigned to the dependent work in progress. The result is, in the best of circumstances, a developer picks up some opportunistic work. The worst result is that work which must be done has to wait because lower-priority work snuck into a gap before it was ready. Figure 7-1 shows a sample work backlog where this blockage silently happens.

	User Story	Story point(s)	Priority
The UI developer cannot start this ➤	As a user, I am able to see my transaction history.	5	1
until the API developer finishes this ➤	As an API consumer, I am able to query a transaction history for a given user.	3	2
so the UI developer grabs this out of order and then has to wait ➤	As a user, I can change text size on the home page.	1	3

Figure 7-1. Flattened dependencies in a work backlog

The Agile Codex addresses and resolves these apparent contradictions in a novel way. It turns out that there are indeed a set of principles and tools which can enable us to organize and manage them efficiently: it is the science of the industrial age assembly line, which evolved to produce the bits of the material world at scale, applied to software development, to produce the bits of the virtual world.

The Codex

Science and Practice

At its core, the Agile Codex is two things:

- An industrial engineering lens on the planning, structuring, and execution of software development work
- Methods of efficient collaboration to achieve this which also encourage strong cross-team relationships

Both of those ingredients, together, ensure that as changes occur during the software development life cycle, a team can respond with agility, optimally minimize uncertainty and risk, clearly see the downstream effects of changes, and transparently respond in the work plan.

Here is the Agile Codex in its simplest terms:

Describe your project as an acyclic dependency tree of sized work items, scoped to be operated on by one software engineer each and completed within a week.

This is the Codex.

Optimally sequence and assign these work items to bring calendar time for delivery as close to effort time as possible. Develop tools and processes to serve the integrity of this dependency tree.

This is the Agile.

© Michael McCormick 2021
M. McCormick, *The Agile Codex*, https://doi.org/10.1007/978-1-4842-7280-0_8

The Codex is highly materialistic on its face. It sets some basic rules about the fundamental atoms of the planning process. The Agile acknowledges, as it always does, that we are people, not tools on an assembly line, and that there will always be disconnects between the map and the territory.

Software engineering is not a rote task – it is primarily a skilled, creative act. As such, we need to account for the space needed to research, plan, create, and adjust. The Agile practices serving the Codex are designed to optimally and efficiently deal with this intersection between the engineering problem of software delivery flow, and the human reality of how work is described, owned, executed, and transitioned from one state to another.

No set of rules will ever anticipate the variety of situations a software delivery experience will encounter. Agile practices must make this adaptation efficient. The Agile practices serving the Codex do this by optimizing the ease at which this adaptation can be codified into the Codex.

At its core, everything an Agile team does must serve the Codex. The creation and the care and feeding of this structured tree of work sets the frame in which all other team actions take place and against which all successes or failures can be evaluated.

The Principles of the Agile Codex

Let us build up the codex from its constituent, primary principles.

Small Units of Work

Small units of work live for a short time in the workflow. They are executed quickly, and their scope of change is small, resulting in quick, low-risk, self-contained, and incremental changes to the code base, which are easy to review and verify.

Breaking down large software engineering tasks to this level also forces the problem into a level of scrutiny that minimizes risks of change and unexpected discovery once the work begins.

The shorter the unit of work lives, the smaller the chance external factors will occur to exert influence or otherwise derail the intent of the work. This means that the lifetime of a piece of work is less likely to be extended by calendar time. In other words, calendar time and effort time are pressured toward unity.

A User Story which is over-sized tends to persist for a long time on the board, with a constant status of "almost done" as it waits for code reviews, rebases against merge conflicts as the base branch changes underneath, and coordination and changes occur as adjacent or conflicting work comes into flight. After getting the code merged, regressions tend to occur as sweeping changes hide edge cases and need to wait for larger scale testing cycles to occur.

Sized

It is easier to estimate the effort required to deliver a small unit of work. Constructing a small item implies understanding the work to be done at a deep enough level that the effort and risks are known and contained. This leads to greater predictability in cumulative workload as this accuracy is summed across the project, with resolution averaging only a couple of days of execution time for the average work item.

If a work item cannot be sized, it is probably not well defined enough to work on.

If a work item cannot be sized, it is probably not well defined enough to work on.

Sequenceable

When the units of work are small, they are easier to define independently of other work, to the extent that the desired and required sequence of their execution can become clear. If one unit depends on another to be completed, the dependency can be indicated. If there is no dependency, then the work can be executed in the optimal order based on sizing and the availability of a given person to work on it.

Attempts to encapsulate dependencies for a User Story as ordered Tasks which are owned across different individuals essentially embeds the life cycle phasing one level below where it should live – at the User Story level, causing confusion as to which life cycle phase the User Story is actually in.

Acyclic Dependency Tree

Sequenceable units of work with clear dependencies can be represented as a dependency tree. The discipline of thinking of work as discrete, small units also helps planners avoid creating accidental circular dependencies, where one piece of work depends on another, which in turn depends on the first.

The construction of the dependency tree from the units of work quickly surfaces any mistaken thinking and planning that may cause cycles in the graph.

Single Owner

Ensuring work is defined in such a way that it can be owned by one single developer throughout the life cycle provides several benefits. The first benefit is that when work is owned by one individual, that individual has clear responsibilities throughout the life cycle of the work which do not change, regardless of the work itself. Second, there is a clear audit trail and connection of one individual to the work described and the work delivered. Lastly, for planning purposes, when one individual can be assigned to each node in the dependency tree, cumulative effort assigned to a given person can be calculated, sequencing can be optimized so no individual is doing too many things at once, and there is a natural push to isolate the scope of work to a single functional area, owing to the fact that individuals tend to have area expertise.

Application

Now that we have identified the principles, we can see how the magic of the Codex is unlocked. These building blocks give us the ability to draw a dependency tree where each node has a time of effort, a set of possible single assignees, and a parent, a child, or neither.

Nodes which have no dependencies can be opportunistically inserted anywhere in the tree.

Figure 8-1 depicts an abstract tree of work nodes.

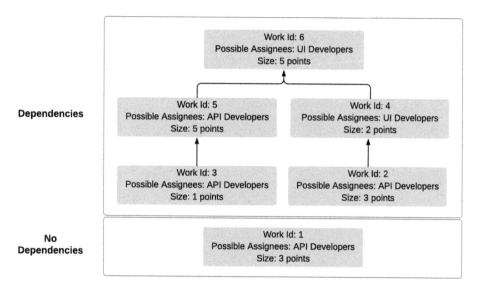

Figure 8-1. Required parameters of a node in a dependency tree. Dependencies are worked from bottom up. Nodes with no Dependencies can be slotted in between any nodes

With the right tooling, we can determine who should own each node, and in which order the nodes should be worked on by each person so that the tree as a whole is delivered in the shortest time possible. And with the translation of effort to time, we have constant visibility of the predicted date of the final deliverable.

As changes occur in the plan during execution, so long as the changes are reflected in the conforming addition, subtraction, or modification of nodes in the tree, we can use our tooling to update the plan by resequencing and reassigning, and immediately have an updated final deliverable date.

The Agile
Map to Territory

The practices we employ to ensure that the nodes in our tree conform to these primary principles are key to the success of the Agile Codex. In this section, I will provide examples of the practices I use. They are by no means dogma, and depending on your organization, business, market, product, and people you may find other, more suitable methods for you.

No matter what you choose to do, the measure of whether a practice is viable is whether or not it serves the integrity of the Codex.

What I have found in my practice is that the rituals, habits, and skills required to serve the integrity of the Codex also serve to build strong individuals and strong, collaborative teams across the business, from product management, design, quality engineering, operations, customer support, marketing, legal, finance, and beyond. The proximal teams are equal shareholders in the maintenance of the codex, with interests aligned toward predictability and achievability, and the business benefits from the increased certainty and visibility provided by the product development group of exactly what is going to be delivered and when.

This level of collaboration and alignment of interests is where the magic of the Codex arises. It is a virtuous spiral of trust where individuals work together to understand the work, characterize the work, and deliver the work with maximum transparency every step of the way.

© Michael McCormick 2021
M. McCormick, *The Agile Codex*, https://doi.org/10.1007/978-1-4842-7280-0_9

Collaboration is key, but collaboration fails when there is no owner or there is ambiguity around how a task is to transition to its next state.

With this in mind, practices work best when they align with the following practice principles.

Clear Ownership of Work at All Times in Each Stage

The single owner principle extends beyond the execution life cycle of a given unit of work, to encompass the definition of the work as well. There must be one shepherd who gathers and synthesizes input, mediates debate, validates the exit criteria to transition the work to the next stage, and records the process.

Clear Inputs

In order for the owner of work in any given stage to gather and build valid input, those inputs need to be defined: what they need to describe, and which people and roles on the team would provide them.

When everyone is speaking the same language, they can speak in common terms about what the problem looks like. The more a team practices this, the more they build the muscle of collaboration. They establish a *cultural template*: an understanding of the set of things they need to worry about and come to agreement on, and how they talk about them.

Clear Transition Criteria

Understanding what must be true to move work from one stage to the next naturally causes work to be defined in a way where that understanding can be achieved. Choosing transition criteria which ensure the integrity of the Codex ensures all parties share a mutual understanding of these key aspects of the work being defined.

A common definition of when work is ready, and how it moves to the next phase, minimizes the churn of anti-directional phase changes when it is realized that something in an earlier phase was missed and the work needs to transition backward in order to be rectified, and then hurdle back forward, or stay in place with a special asterisk and out-of-band to-do item for the responsible party.

Clear Outputs

What work must look like when it transitions is also critical. When transition criteria are clear, it is natural and simple to record their values in an explicit, auditable, and understandable way, embodied in the transformation of the information describing the work. Like relay racers handing off the baton, the work is immediately actionable in the next stage, the same way, every time.

Stakeholder Approval

While one owner is responsible for delivering the work to the next stage, it is critical that the assertions of the values of the transition criteria are understood and agreed to by all stakeholders before the work transitions. Viewing the work from their interests in representing either the quality of their inputs, if they are upstream, or the requirements of their inputs if they are downstream, each stakeholder must sign-off that the transition criteria have been met from their point of view.

This right of veto not only ensures that the work has been properly examined, the auditing of the sign-off ensures there is a paper trail to expose gaps if things do not go as expected.

Benefits

Predictability, Speed, Quality

When the Agile Codex principles are practiced, teams gain both a shared understanding of what they are building in specifics as well as what defining that work requires. Each member of the team becomes an expert in fitting their piece of the puzzle in place.

This expertise, combined with the democratic process of stakeholder approval means that the systems can evolve. As exceptions arise, and pieces do not neatly fit, the team is prepared to discuss and evolve the practices from a common frame of reference.

The principles of the Codex can be the guides of how best to modify the practice – that is, how to adjust the transition criteria and measures, or inputs, or outputs, to better create a cohesive node in the Codex.

The result is an efficiently evolvable phase transition system, able to withstand occasional one-offs and absorb new policies and practices without disrupting the core reason that it all works.

Low Overhead

With the proper tooling in place to represent, optimize, manage, and audit the history of the dependency graph, and proper processes in place to maintain its integrity, the practical overhead is minimal.

© Michael McCormick 2021

M. McCormick, *The Agile Codex*, https://doi.org/10.1007/978-1-4842-7280-0_10

Each person understands their roles and responsibilities, and the occasional situations which require extending beyond quickly become clear. The atomic habits of work hygiene surface in strong commitments to the integrity of the process as a whole.

Most importantly, delegation of responsibility to each contributor and owner distributes intelligence and effort evenly into the system, unburdening project managers from complex dependency status tracking. Individuals describe their work and its adjacent dependencies. The tooling surfaces the entire tree, and the project manager applies the science and art to choose the optimal scenario. No single person needs to know everything in order for the machinery to synchronously hum along.

A clean and visible work tree also provides a consistent picture and sense of ownership and visibility of progress to the team as a whole. My teams have found this a self-reinforcing reward loop – they see firsthand the benefit of the codex and are encouraged to do their part to take care of it.

Detailed Auditing

Having a picture of the work tree through time opens up many avenues for metrics and auditing. Every time it changes, the source of change is clear, be it a shift in dependencies, a mistake or miscommunication in planning, a change in external or internal dependencies, the addition or removal of nodes, and any unexpected changes in the calendar lifetime of a node.

Bottlenecks also become immediately apparent, along with their effects on the final delivery date. Adjustments to the plan can be made on the spot, and good judgments can be made early on how to mitigate, from removal of work from the tree to reassignment and resequencing to re-minimize gaps in the execution timelines.

On the positive side, work completing early offers another chance to rebalance, pulling in more work opportunistically, or otherwise taking advantage of breathing room.

The codex also provides visibility to external teams who are dependent on delivery of work. Knowing the predicted day each node is expected to be delivered allows them to plan their own resources accordingly, to be ready to receive the completed work, knowing what it is going to be, and to fit it into their own work plans. Knowing immediately when that predicted day changes maximizes lead time to adjust dependent plans.

Quick and Safe Deliveries

The short lifetime and discrete containment of change in each work item allows the team as a whole to provide demonstrably working code early and often. Code reviews are fast, and developers learn to think about their deliverables proactively and to conceptualize their work in discrete, independent units. This develops an uncanny ability to think deeply and efficiently about the architecture and implementation from an early stage.

Many Quality Gates

The democratic work development and transition model provides implicit quality gates to each step of the process. With many eyes, each tuned to their areas of expertise, reviewing and approving or pausing the progress of the work through the life cycle, divergences and miscommunications are caught long before they become issues, or worse, catastrophes.

From Invention to Assembly Line

Building the Tree

The Agile Codex emphasizes strict dependency identification and tracking. Why is this so important?

The Importance of Dependencies

The fundamental question in any project always comes down to "What is going to be delivered, and when?" Arriving at the truest answer to this question is the holy grail of all collaborative building projects. Imagine a conversation with a few tradespersons building a home:

"Charlie, When will those two boards be nailed together?"

M. McCormick, *The Agile Codex*, https://doi.org/10.1007/978-1-4842-7280-0_11

"Two minutes (assuming the hammer hits the nail on the head and the boards stay true)."

"Ana, when will this wall be framed?"

"Three hours (assuming the studs were nailed together as planned (assuming the hammer hits the nail on the head and the boards stay true))."

"Jack, when will the house be framed?"

"5 days (assuming the walls were framed as planned (assuming the studs were nailed together as planned (assuming the hammer hits the nail on the head and the boards stay true)))."

At each level, the "what" that is being delivered changes. Everyone along the chain of delivery asks for their "what." And sometimes, when they worry, they ask for the "whats" before that, and before those:

"Are you sure the frame will be done in 5 days, Ana? What about the kitchen wall, Jack? Will Ana really get it in time?"

Depending on the level you look, not only does the answer but the question changes as well. At the micro level, we are asking "When will those two boards be nailed together?" One level higher: "When will this wall be framed?" Another level: "When will the house be framed?" until finally: "When can we move in?"

At each higher level, the answer becomes loaded down with more and more assumptions.

So, the answer is always, "it depends," meaning, it is critical that at any level it is easy to unroll those dependencies to both calculate and justify the answer.

Sometimes the "what" is more important than the "when," such as we often see in the video game industry, or with Apple hardware releases, where rumors of and actual delays are the norm.

Sometimes the "when" takes primacy, especially in emerging software startups, where Minimum Viable Product is the goal, and first customers have the expectation that they will be beta users for a long time.

Sometimes neither matters, as in the world of experimentation and research into emerging or not-yet-existing markets, such as Alphabet's X – the moonshot factory.

Both "what" *and* "when" are important in large projects with many interdependencies and cross-team collaboration, where delays and bugs can have significant cascading upstream and downstream effects as you might see in the enterprise software industry and high-technology-equipment manufacturing.

No matter which variant you see, the basic truth behind it all is that

- Every assumption is a dependency.
- Every dependency is a risk.
- Every risk has a cost.

Planning and executing the delivery of software is the art of minimizing that cost, which means identifying, classifying, and minimizing risk throughout the life cycle by correctly identifying and tracking dependencies.

Building the Assembly Line

Now a thought exercise to draw a (literal) picture of what the Codex means in practice: we will build a saltshaker.

In the physical world, the order of operations is largely obvious, thanks to gravity. In order to build up, you must root down. No roof can be placed on a home without walls. No walls can be placed on soil without a foundation. While some things can be built in parallel, and stitched together all at once, the full assemblage can never exist out of order.

So to make these dependencies obvious, let us start with an example in the physical world. Consider the saltshaker. A ubiquitous, unassuming resident of every kitchen and restaurant table. What is it made of?

Simply:

A base that holds salt, and a lid with holes in it.

Let us break that down a bit more.

The base is hollow. It is light enough to be picked up with one hand. It may be transparent, allowing one to see how much salt is inside. It may have ridges, or texture to ensure a secure grip while shaking. The top is threaded to secure a removable lid. The base is flat, to keep it upright. It has enough volume to store many shakes of salt. The lid has holes in it, of just the right diameter to let some grains pass when inverted, but not too many. And there are enough of these holes that every shake accumulates enough salt to mitigate the need for too many shakes when seasoning a typical plate.

As the inventive humans we are, we imagine the construction of this saltshaker. We invent it backward by detailing its physical components in their final form:

The base is a hollow cylinder of ridged glass, threaded at the top. The lid is stainless steel, perforated on top, and threaded to the size of the base.

And imagine backward thus:

The lid: Given a steel disc, shape it into a lid. Thread the lid and poke holes in the lid.

The base: Given glass, shape it into a hollow cylinder. Thread the glass at the top of the cylinder.

Assembly: Screw the lid onto the base.

It is helpful now to draw the nouns of the process described above as they change through time (Figure 11-1).

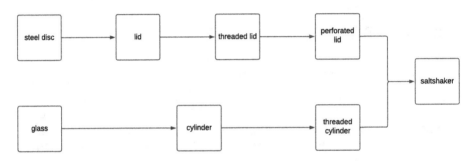

Figure 11-1. Ordered stages of assembly

And connect them with the verbs (Figure 11-2).

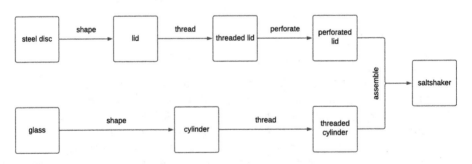

Figure 11-2. Actions on the ordered stages of assembly

And now we have our simplified assembly line.

Our verbs are actions being performed on the nouns. Actions require tools, so let us make that explicit (Figure 11-3).

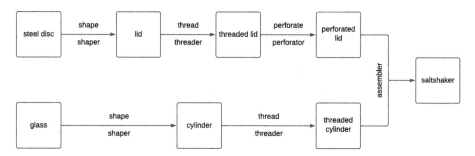

Figure 11-3. Tools and their actions on the ordered stages of assembly

Every tool takes a certain amount of time to do its work – to transform the object from one state to another. And some states take a tool longer to transform than others. In our case, it turns out that threading a glass cylinder takes two minutes, while threading a steel disc takes three.

Let us next indicate how long each step takes via the length of the line (Figure 11-4).

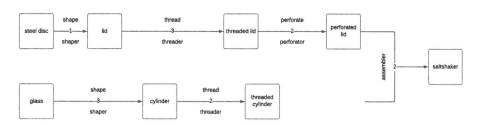

Figure 11-4. Time for each transformation

Threading and perforating of our lid could happen in either order, so we have a second option for this assembly line where we flip the order of those two steps (Figure 11-5).

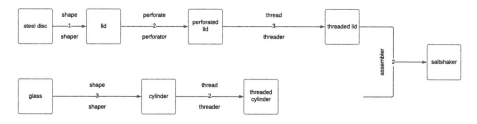

Figure 11-5. Alternate order: perforate lid before threading

Based on this, how long does it take to build our saltshaker?

The obvious answer is eight: the longest cumulative line. This cumulative line is our calendar time. And it turns out, making the lid takes longer than making the base. The lid is our *gating factor*. In fact, our cylinder is waiting for one minute before the lid is ready to be assembled to it (Figure 11-6).

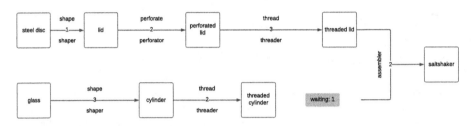

Figure 11-6. Cylinder waiting for one minute while lid completes

Pretty simple and straightforward so far, right? Now let us complicate it.

It turns out our factory can only afford one threader and one shaper! What this means is that we can neither shape nor thread two different parts simultaneously. Figure 11-7 shows the overlap in our original assembly scenarios where the same tool would be in simultaneous use.

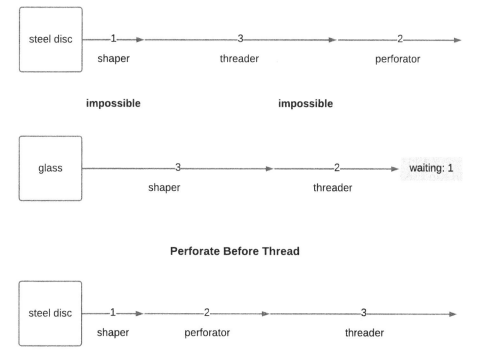

Thread Before Perforate

Perforate Before Thread

Figure 11-7. Cylinder waiting for one minute while lid completes

Now that we have our assembly line, and this new constraint where the same tool cannot be used simultaneously, how can we parallelize the work to minimize the calendar time spent (indicated by the length left to right)?

Goal   Parallelize the work to minimize calendar time.

Reviewing our constraints:

- Time to perform each step.
- Required sequence of steps.
- No steps requiring the threader or shaper can happen concurrently.

Now play out each possible scenario (removing the final assembly step which is common to each).

Figure 11-8 depicts the first scenario, where we thread the lid before perforating it, and delay using the shaper for the cylinder one minute so the lid can use it first. The calendar time (length of the longest set of lines, left to right) is 6, effort time (total time tools are in use) is 11, and idle time (the amount of time a tool is not available for a task which uses it) is 1.

Scenario 1

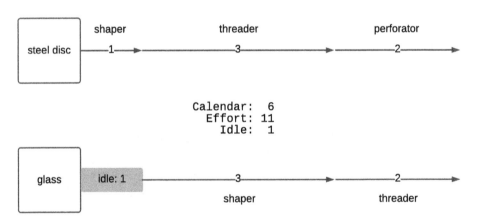

Figure 11-8. Delaying the use of the shaper in constructing the cylinder when threading the lid before perforating the lid

In the second scenario (Figure 11-9), still threading the lid before perforating, we instead choose to delay the use of the shaper tool on the lid, which causes us to also need to delay the use of the threader tool while the cylinder finishes using it. The calendar time in this scenario is 10, effort time is still 11, and idle time is 9. The cylinder assembly line sits idle for a whopping 5 minutes while the lid is completed.

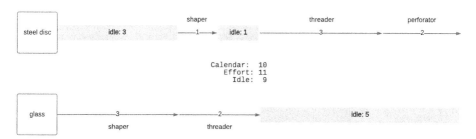

Figure 11-9. Delaying the use of the shaper and threader in constructing the lid when thread-ing the lid before perforating the lid

In the third scenario (Figure 11-10), we switch the order of threading and perforating of the lid, which removes 1 minute of idle time from Scenario 2 as we no longer have simultaneous need to use the threader on each line. This reduces our calendar time to 9, effort time is the same at 11, and idle time reduces by 2, as not only do we not need to wait for the threader tool on the cylinder line, but we also finish a minute earlier, so the cylinder line waits less time before it can start again on the next saltshaker.

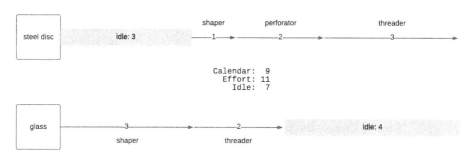

Figure 11-10. Delaying the use of the shaper and threader in constructing the lid when per-forating the lid before threading the lid

In the fourth scenario (Figure 11-11), we shape the disc first (as in Scenario 1). Now the threader is operating on the lid after the perforator, so the lid waits on the cylinder assembly to finish with the threader before it can be threaded. Finally, the cylinder waits for the lid to complete. This scenario has no change to calendar time, effort time, or idle time compared with Scenario 3.

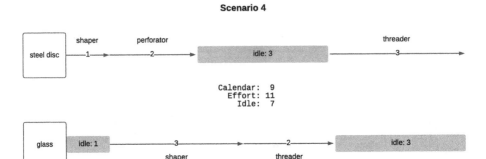

Figure 11-11. Delaying the use of the shaper and threader in constructing the cylinder when perforating the lid before threading the lid

In these scenarios, we have sequencing which is forced by dependencies:

- Cylinder shaping must happen before threading.
- Lid shaping must happen before perforating and threading.

And sequencing alternatives:

- Lid could be perforated before threading.
- Lid could be threaded before perforating.

In each scenario, we count the

- Calendar time: The total time for the saltshaker parts to be complete
- Effort time: The total time spent doing work before the saltshaker is complete
- Idle time: The time work is not happening before the saltshaker is complete

Scenario 1 has the fewest gaps, or least idle time possible, at 1, and also has the shortest calendar time, at 6. Scenario 1 is the optimal choice.

In Review

We imagined our saltshaker backward into a series of transformational steps, identifying

- Which steps could happen in either order
- Which steps could not
- How long each step takes
- Which steps use the same tool

Once we identified the possible dependency trees, we were able to play out scenarios until finding the optimal solution.

This same mechanistic process of optimizing the assembly applies just as well to our software assembly line. As with our saltshaker, all software delivery methodologies are dependent upon how well the end product can be envisioned and broken into discrete, sized, and sequenced tasks, which are then optimally parallelized across shared resources.

If anything causes the tree to change, we can simply reconstruct the new tree and replay scenarios as above, choose the optimal one, and resequence our assembly line to reflect it.

In this book we will move this saltshaker analogy into the software world, making the case for the effectiveness and feasibility of this platonic ideal, and how we can best approach it in a variety of circumstances. Because it turns out that doing this well, in the right way, not only maximizes certainty around what will be delivered by when, it also minimizes the cost of the inevitable: change.

Team Functions
The Tree Builders

We have talked about ownership and democratic contribution to development and transition of nodes in the tree. In these examples, we will consider each functional area below a contributing team, with a description of their roles. They will be largely familiar to anyone involved in the business of software. The acronyms will be used throughout the remainder of this book to refer to each respective team.

User Experience (UX)

Responsible for designing the user interface, which generally includes user research, high-level interface flows, information architecture, page design, typography and styling, and graphic design.

Product Management (PM)

Defines the product to be delivered in terms of broad product vision, distilled to specific customer requirements.

© Michael McCormick 2021
M. McCormick, *The Agile Codex*, https://doi.org/10.1007/978-1-4842-7280-0_12

Engineering Management (EM)

Interchangeable term for project manager, scrum master, planner, and leader of DEV.

Development (DEV)

Software engineers who write the code.

Quality Engineering (QE)

Responsible for ensuring the quality of the product through planning and testing before delivery.

Documentation (DOC)

Communicates with the end user on how to use the software, from broad manuals to user interface word choices to help text.

Operations (OPS)

Manages all technical aspects of building and deploying software to various environments. Provides services for continuous integration and delivery as well as operational tooling and management interfaces.

Customer Support Group (CSG)

Manages customer interaction, providing technical support and handling investigations and customer escalations. CSG is a critical part of the feedback loop to product development as the voice of the customer, feeding bugs and feature requests back into the development life cycle based on customer experiences.

In addition to specific requests on behalf of customers, CSG is uniquely positioned to inform engineering of patterns of issues and challenges customers face while using the product. As such, CSG can also play a part in the planning and grooming process for all product features which will need to be supported on behalf of customers.

While the functional boundaries and described duties above may vary in any given organization, this segmentation best illustrates the immediate functional contributors into and out of the software assembly line and will serve as the baseline for the following practical illustrations.

Software Development Life Cycle

Growing the Tree

The software development life cycle (SDLC) describes the workflow of planning, executing, and packaging a software product for delivery.

Phases

The software development life cycle consists of three stages of varying length and complexity:

- Planning
- Execution
- Releasing

© Michael McCormick 2021
M. McCormick, *The Agile Codex*, https://doi.org/10.1007/978-1-4842-7280-0_13

Planning

During the planning phase, all functional areas gather to define what they want to build during the SDLC. Together, they define the saltshaker, and then imagine it backward. The assembly line is put in place: states, steps, and tools are identified, the dependency tree is built, efforts of each transformation are estimated and resourced, and the optimal sequence is defined.

Execution

During the execution phase, the assembly line runs. Work flows through the board. Changes in plan are incorporated and the dependency tree is rebuilt, re-sequenced, and reassigned as needed to accommodate and maintain optimization. Execution can be continuous (e.g., Kanban and continuous delivery) or chunked (multiple sprints and sprint deliveries).

Releasing

During the releasing phase, the final verification and packaging of the product is completed, and the product is prepared for delivery to the customer (Figure 13-1).

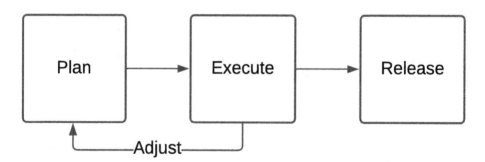

Figure 13-1. SDLC phases

Choosing a Cadence

The life cycle cadence refers to how long each phase takes, as well as how many times a part of the cycle is repeated. For example, some releases involve multiple Sprints, each of which is a mini *plan / execute / release* while other approaches may repeat the *execute / plan* cycle several times before the release phase. The cadence that makes sense depends on many factors.

In enterprise markets, especially, where sales cycles are long, and technology adoption can be slow and expensive, customers need clear expectations of what is coming, and time to prepare and resources to absorb it. Providers of enterprise software need to allocate, train, and mobilize marketing, finance, sales, distribution, legal, and support staff to be ready to serve the needs of the business and customer once the software is delivered. All of this takes time and predictability.

An enterprise software company may release several major updates per year. While still lightning fast in the enterprise world, this rate is glacially slow compared with the update cycle for a consumer app such as Facebook, which may happen as often as every other day.

In these two examples, it is easy to identify the need for stability and predictability versus the need to constantly experiment with, respond to, and even drive consumer tastes and trends.

So, while it is true that the primary release track for these particular projects is indeed reflected in the cadence of their software development life cycles, it is also true that parallel tracks around infrastructural support and longer-term experiments happen at consumer-focused companies like Facebook and innovative, faster-moving feature pilots happen frequently in the enterprise software space.

How SDLC Length Affects Practices

The shorter life cycles can be described well in the two-week Agile paradigm in its purest form: light planning every two weeks, continuous deployment and delivery after execution, and plenty of room to pivot even within the cycle. Projects can even be planned, adjusted, and delivered continuously using a multi-conveyor-belt-like Kanban approach.

The longer life cycles break a release into sprints, where requirements and release goals are debated, sized, and planned for execution across multiple sprints. Technical risk is mitigated with design spikes during planning. Product risk is mitigated through iteration and collaboration across stakeholders, with strong alignments and commitments to deadlines and sometimes even purchasing commitments from customers.

The extreme version of the long cycle is typically referred to as "waterfall," which referred originally to multi-year software releases of the pre-cloud, pre-Internet, install-from-a-box, or embed-on-a-chip days. This approach is still highly effective and necessary in some industries, especially those manufacturing large and expensive machinery and hardware to government and industry under detailed, multi-million (or even billion) dollar contracts.

When the rapid iteration and seamless distribution model of Internet and cloud arrived, the Agile revolution threw off those chains of lugubrious and unnecessary overhead for most software developers.

We can imagine two poles of Agile, with each being defined around how and when we plan compared with how and when we deliver. As in the Consumer versus Enterprise examples, each project has a different amount of planning needed and possible based on how far ahead product requirements and technical risks can be envisioned.

In the traditional sprint-based Agile (Sprint Agile), work for the release begins immediately, with requirements defined, and user stories constructed shortly before coding begins, often on a two-week basis. As the two weeks wind down, coding work trends back down in favor of planning for the next two weeks. This approach is biased toward learning by doing and showing, and the frequent, brief planning cycles can allow for strong, quick pivots.

In its pure form, each sprint is considered a terminal release, and all sprint metrics are geared toward measuring effectiveness of delivering the planned features into a verified and shippable product.

Tacking one sprint to another, the share of planning and coding in each cycle looks something like this (Figure 13-2).

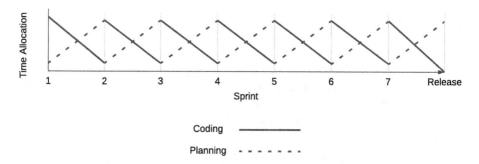

Figure 13-2. Sprint Agile time allocations between planning and coding

When a particular feature might take several sprints to build, it is also planned, largely in pieces, during those pre-sprint planning cycles. User Stories are planned and appear just before sprints begin.

For software projects where any release requires multiple sprints, the planning curve can be more flexible (Figure 13-3). Because this approach starts with planning for the *release* more in the beginning, we can call it Release Agile.

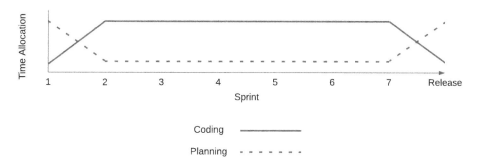

Figure 13-3. Release Agile time allocations between planning and coding

With effective up-front planning (before the work begins in earnest) the need to adjust and re-plan around sprint boundaries goes down. Execution can continue without as much cyclic context switching into planning mode. User Stories live for many sprints, and only enter the sprints when the time is right according to the dependency tree scenario in play at the time.

Again, this investment in a long-lived User Story is only worth making when the User Stories conform to the Codex and can be efficiently shuffled and optimized every time the situation, the dependency tree, changes.

It makes sense in the traditional sprint model that we would not want to invest in long-term planning, as that model presumes that shuffling is expensive. As the cost of that shuffling goes up, so does the cost of mis-planning and therefore, by definition, learning. Any system which treats learning as expensive incentivizes its opposite.

Any system which treats learning as expensive incentivizes its opposite.

In high-risk, experimental projects, the re-planning between each execution cycle can be more involved as it focuses on absorbing the new knowledge. On projects of higher certainty, re-planning can be much lighter. In other words, high-certainty projects are more amenable to investing in up-front planning.

Sometimes the experimental nature of a project is more or less than expected. So, we also need to have mechanisms in place to identify this and adjust the level and type of planning we are doing even within the project life cycle. The primary mechanism here is what I call "requirements escape" – where planning incorrectly assumed something was true which was not or was unable to identify a first-level risk. Every planning cycle must spend time evaluating the unexpected work uncovered while learning during the execution phase and track that trend in order to properly allocate time for changing cycle times or increasing inter-cycle planning when needed.

Constructing the Codex

In order to identify what we do not know, we first inventory what we do know.

In this phase, it is most critical to involve the community of contributors. No one brain knows everything. PM and UX think through the user experience, translate it to interface flows, DEV thinks through how it might be built, QE thinks through how it might be tested, OPS offers how it might be packaged and deployed, and DOC tries to explain what they are. Through this iterative discussion and negotiation of the knowns, the unknowns – the risks – are also set in stark relief.

As with the saltshaker, we start with a broad vision of the product: a proposal, often with business justification, which goes through the experience we wish the user to have with the product. From there, PM and UX collaborate to imagine the user interfaces and flows which would be needed to support this vision. During this collaboration, they challenge assumptions, perform thought experiments, draw things up, shoot things down, uncover questions that need answering, and refine the vision.

Once this vision has narrowed into a set of high-level requirement statements, given in the language of the user experience (as "use cases"), the rest of the team comes together to clarify, debate, discuss, and redefine the requirements, which often leads to revisions to UX as well. The output of this process is engineering User Stories which address how a specific use case or part of a use case will be addressed in the form of software code.

These User Stories include estimates of effort time and required dependencies on or for other User Stories. These User Stories are sized small enough to be completed, reviewed, and put into the main product code with minimal risk or disruption. This small size also helps force them into clear boundary statements where dependencies do not end up in cycles – that is, where one piece of a work item depends on a piece in another User Story which in turn depends back on another task in the original User Story. Also, by keeping the tasks constrained to one particular skill set or expertise, they can be owned by one single resource during execution.

These User Stories are the sized and sequenced nodes in our acyclic dependency tree.

User Stories are the sized and sequenced nodes in our acyclic dependency tree.

In this manner, the project can be envisioned in terms of sequence (required, and flexible), possible assignees, and effort time for each User Story. Thinking back to our saltshaker, we can draw the possible dependency trees, identify the shared tooling (the set of developers with the required skill to do the task), draw the length of the line (the required time as effort), and optimize the assembly line to the shortest possible calendar time.

At this point, there is no prescribed sequence, assignee, or order. Just the universe of possibilities constrained by our known dependencies. But this is not enough to decide on the optimal scenario. There is one more factor to help us choose: risk.

Risk Management

Science and Mitigation

When we talk about risk, we are primarily talking about the risk of incurring greater effort time than planned, because anything which causes our plan to require more effort time also may also cost calendar time. When our delivery date for a given commitment moves out, we either need to adjust the commitment (compromise on feature or quality), or we need to adjust the commitment date (deliver later).

Categories of Risk

Let us look at four principal categories of risk as they relate to software development, each impacting when and how the planning to minimize them is best done.

© Michael McCormick 2021

M. McCormick, *The Agile Codex*, https://doi.org/10.1007/978-1-4842-7280-0_14

Product Risk: How Clearly and Comprehensively the Product Can Be Defined

Quickly building something in order to see it, get feedback on it, from internal businesspeople or customers, facilitates conversation and helps articulate requirements when they may be challenging to pull from whole cloth.

Technical Risk: How Clearly and Comprehensively It Is Understood How to Build It

Software engineering is as much, if not more, of a creative art as an engineering skill. Tools and technologies evolve. They require constant learning and evaluation. Architectures evolve in turn. And at the leading edge is invention – finding a new optimization, a new combination of parts and sequences, to strike algorithmic gold.

Market Risk: Any Demand-Side Shift Which Creates an Arbitrage Opportunity for a Quick Feature Pivot

For example, a competitor builds a better mousetrap, so you change to a rat trap. Or a global pandemic halves demand in your primary market while doubling it in the adjacent one. The key concept is these are changes outside of your organization in the demand for the product you have planned.

Business Risk: Any Supply-Side Shift Which Creates an Arbitrage Opportunity for a Quick Feature Pivot

You can think of business risk as any activities inside the organization which affect the resourcing, timing of delivery, or dependencies of a software project. Surprises can be on the upside, such as hiring more people, or the downside, such as layoffs. These can affect your team or adjacent teams, impacting when business units can absorb your delivery, or when your external dependencies can be met. The key concept here is these are changes in your ability to supply the planned product due to changes inside your organization.

Today and Tomorrow Risk

We can further group these risks in terms of *Today* and *Tomorrow* risk.

Product and technical risk are risks which relate to the information that exists, but we do not have. These are *Today* risks.

Market and business risk relates to the information that does not exist today but might one day. These are *Tomorrow* risks.

We can mitigate Today risk by learning. We learn as we go, or more accurately, we go, in order to learn. The less you know, the more important it is to break work into discrete feature experiments, delivered quickly, as each full pass through the execution cycle presents an opportunity to experiment and learn. For product risk, this enables more frequent feedback on the design and functionality, with less investment sunk into any misalignment. For technical risk, this enables the opportunity to prototype and pivot, without the need to invest in grand abstractions and frameworks before testing the value of the investment they would support.

We learn as we go, or more accurately, we go, in order to learn.

We can be proactive with Tomorrow risk through *invention*: intentionally attempting to create things that will benefit us but did not exist before.

Lastly, we can be reactive toward Tomorrow risk through *resilience*. The best thing we can do in the face of external uncertainty is to be adaptable to the most likely sets of events we can imagine.

Fortunately, the prescription is the same here as it is for product and technical risk. If you break work into discrete feature experiments, delivered quickly, you have made investments optimally based on knowledge you have, and can pivot while throwing away less.

Positive Interactions with Risk

Figure 14-1 depicts these risk categories and how we can create positive interactions with them.

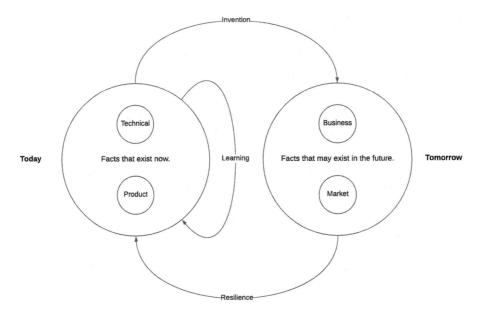

Figure 14-1. Risk categories and how we create positive interaction

While the structure of your work may be the same in both cases, the planning you do in each category is different. We mitigate Today risk by planning our work in an order that optimizes learning. We mitigate Tomorrow risk by prioritizing technologies and processes that can flex to support the most likely changes, and by having the tools in place to adjust on the fly.

In simplistic terms, planning and execution are competing resources. They both take from the common pool of time. Time spent doing one is time not spent doing the other.

Where one activity is a perfect substitute for the other, one hour taken from one is one fewer hour one can do the other.

At any given point in *time*, this is most certainly true.

It is our good fortune in software development that planning and execution are not perfect substitutes when considered through time. Good planning minimizes the right risks, thereby minimizing the cost of the unexpected.

How you do one affects how much you need to do of the other, over time. It is in this interplay where the process science of software development yields its reward.

There is an optimal balance between planning and execution where, over time, the right planning allows more work to be done in a given time, not less. If you spend all day planning you never have time to do, and if you spend all day doing without a plan, you waste the time you have.

Risk Quadrants and Risk over Time

In order to understand which risks we *should* minimize, we need to understand a little bit more about risk. Risks can be categorized along the axes of cost and likelihood (Figure 14-2).

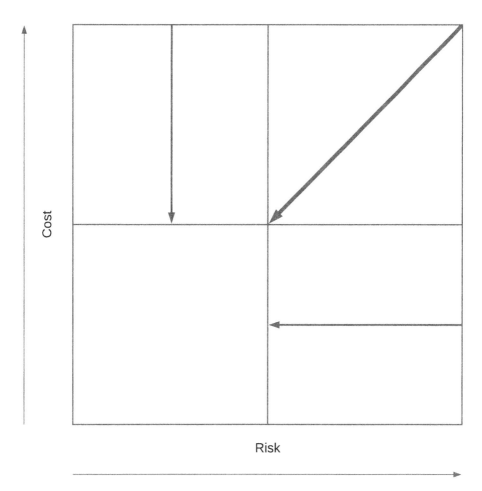

Figure 14-2. The quadrants of risk

The obvious quadrant to minimize is high-cost, high-likelihood events, while the opposite quadrant of low-cost, low-likelihood events is the least worrisome. The low-likelihood, high-cost quadrant is the target for insurance companies, where loss would be catastrophic, and the high-likelihood, low-cost quadrant matters more the more events there are which reside in it.

But this is not enough to tell us what to do. There is another vector which will help us understand which actual risks we should focus on besides expected cost, and that is the cost of mitigation: there is a cost to moving a risk to a lower quadrant.

In planning, our goal is to identify the risks which can be moved, and the cost of moving them. Imagining this movement of risks introduces our third dimension, which is time. Risks can move in this space of their own accord or through our intentions over time.

For each risk we identify, we need to classify it: Can it be moved? Then assess not only what it would cost to move, which we understand by identifying the actions we would need to take to move it.

Planning allows us to think through the risk space and do this identification and classification. It is the art of seeing through the life cycle of the risk and how we can most efficiently learn and thereby move the risk to a lower space on the graph.

You can imagine each point on the graph has mass, and the larger the mass, the more time (effort) it takes to move. You can further imagine that as it moves, its mass can change – some things that are easy to mitigate in the beginning can be more difficult later in the project, and vice versa.

With careful planning, we can map out this life cycle with some level of clarity. The more experimental the problem, the less deep our vision can be, and the more the bets we make on where risks will move become risky themselves.

While all this seems quite complex and may feel overwhelming, in practice we can focus on a simple set of guidelines.

First, just understand that learning is nothing but basic scientific experimentation:

- Hypothesize (plan)
- Test (execute)

Once we know what we do not know, for our coming execution phase, we can prioritize the risks which are

- Highest cost to course-correct if assumptions turn out wrong (the "mass" of the risk goes up over time)
- Easiest to mitigate (the "mass" of the risk is low today)

And then order them in the execution plan by how they and the next level of risks would be affected by solving them.

Given these priorities, when choosing between dependency graphs for our assembly line, we can promote the trees which move our higher-priority risks to higher consideration.

Planning for Resilience

We can build into our plan a buffer for risky areas. Looking at our scenarios, any time there is idle time is time where two types of discovered effort can be spent:

- Extra effort required to complete the preceding work

- Any work which has no child dependencies that is not already complete

---

Idle time can be used as a buffer for discovered work.

Recall Scenario 4 (Figure 14-3).

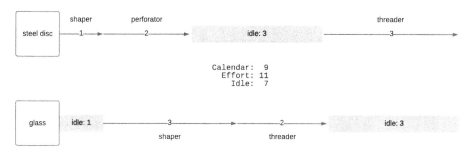

Figure 14-3. Scenario 4 with perforator having 3 minutes of idle time immediately after it

Imagine that the perforation task for the lid took three more hours. There would be no impact to the plan: the task would simply run into the idle time. This is an example of the first type (see Figure 14-4).

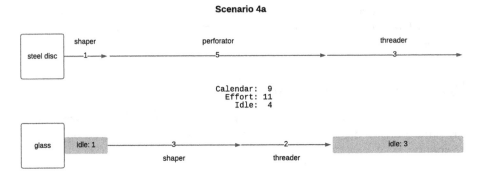

Figure 14-4. Scenario 4 modified with perforator time extended from 2 to 5 minutes, using the 3 minutes of idle time which was originally immediately after it

The second type reflects how we can opportunistically use idle time. Every idle minute in a scenario could be for opportunistic work which does not have a child dependency that is not yet complete. Figure 14-5 depicts how this would surface in our Scenario 4 workflow.

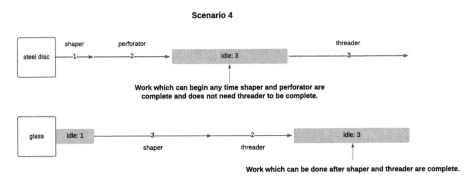

Figure 14-5. Places where independent and uncompleted work can be done

What you can see here is that opportunistic work and the imperfect ability to fill in all gaps can be turned into a benefit as a project is underway. While we always want to eliminate the gaps as we plan forward, it is true that gaps are unavoidable as are unexpected changes. When those changes occur, the gaps can occasionally become advantages – significant re-sequencing can be avoided if a change falls into one of the two categories above and a properly sized gap can be used.

In our saltshaker scenarios, we had two sequencing options – perforate then thread the lid, or thread, then perforate. Imagine that there is a chance the perforation tool will break the lid, causing us to need to start over. We do not know for sure that it will break the lid, but it might.

In that case, we may prefer to prioritize the sequence of perforation before threading in order to be able to learn as quickly as possible and, in the case that it breaks the lid, start over. We would, in this case, prioritize any scenarios where the perforation happens as soon as possible. Scenario 4 (Figure 14-6) would be preferred to Scenario 1 (Figure 14-7), even though it reflects a longer calendar time in the perfect scenario, because in the imperfect scenario, replanning would be possible sooner in the lifetime of the work.

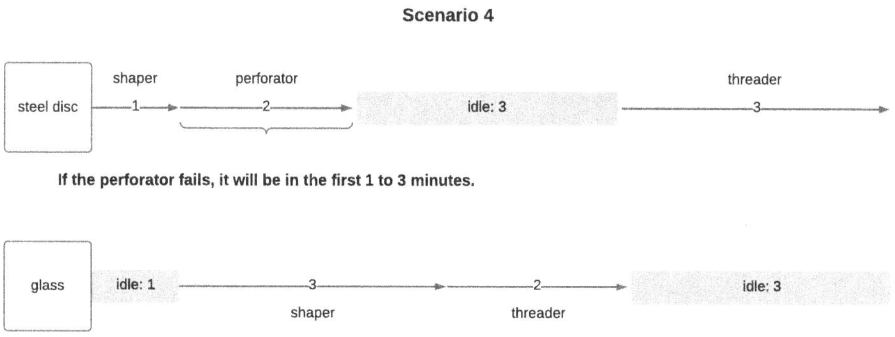

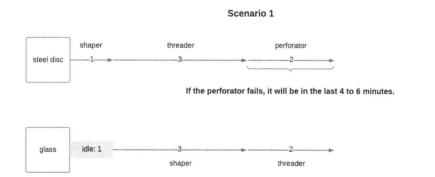

Figure 14-6. Failure mitigation can happen within the first 1–3 minutes in Scenario 4

Figure 14-7. Failure mitigation cannot happen until the last 4–6 minutes in Scenario 1

In order to demonstrate how we replan, let us have the perforation step fail after the first hour, ruining the lid, while our cylinder is one hour into its shaping. We need to restart the lid and cannot do it until the cylinder shaper tool becomes available. We can see there are idle blocks in both lines at the same time, which we can eliminate by pulling the threading tool to start right after the perforation tool (Figure 14-8).

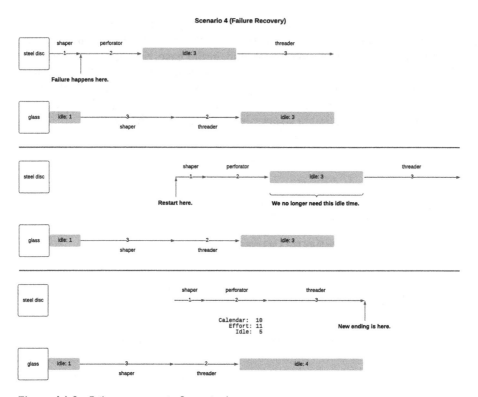

Figure 14-8. Failure recovery in Scenario 4

Being able to visualize allows us to identify these opportunities and replan to minimize calendar time and adjust our committed delivery time immediately after the lid breaks (two hours in). The total calendar time ends up being ten hours.

If we had chosen our Scenario 1, we would find out five hours into construction and need to restart. Adjusting the plan at that point results in total calendar time reaching eleven hours (Figure 14-9).

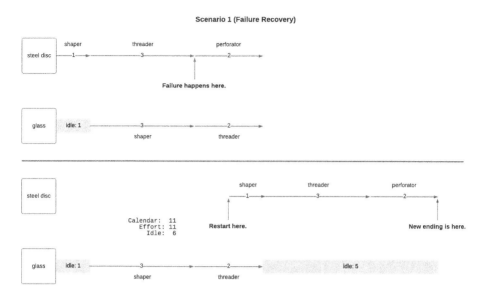

Figure 14-9. Failure recovery in Scenario 1

Here we see the science of risk mitigation at work. We did not know if our perforating tool would work, so by choosing Scenario 4, we prioritize finding that out early, in order to be able to quickly and efficiently adjust the plan. When we had the choice about a sequence, we chose to mitigate risk – to learn by doing – and fail early in order to recover quickly.

When we chose Scenario 4, we chose to execute in order to bring future facts into being. By comparing Scenarios 4 and 1, we were able to evaluate the cost / benefit of the lid breaking and make a choice to minimize that risk.

When we chose Scenario 4 (increasing time from 9 to 10 minutes) over Scenario 1 (increasing time from 6 to 11 minutes), we chose to move the risk of the lid breaking to a lower quadrant. The cost of choosing Scenario 4 in the case the lid did not break is 3 – choosing 9 minutes over 6. The payoff of choosing Scenario 4 in the case the lid *did* break was 1 – choosing 10 minutes over 11.

So, we decided that it is worth spending 3 minutes in order to potentially save 1 minute. We also decided that we were willing to pay for a smaller *range* of risk at the same time – in the case of Scenario 4, a range of 1 (either 9 or 10), and in the case of Scenario 1, a range of 5 (either 6 or 11).

We can look at the range in our quadrant as the risk – the higher the range, the greater the risk. If it is worth 3 minutes to have a risk of 1 instead of 5 then we choose Scenario 4.

Conclusion

Because we learn as we go, and we can neither predict, control, nor mitigate every risk, change will happen. Markets may demand something else, we may hire or lose a team member, we may discover a software tool is not what we expected, and so on. Because this is true, it must be inexpensive to change.

By prioritizing the risks which are

- Highest cost to course-correct if assumptions turn out wrong (the "mass" of the risk goes up over time)

- And easiest to mitigate (the "mass" of the risk is low today)

we can promote the trees which move our higher-priority risks to higher consideration.

We did this in our examples by choosing to prioritize Scenario 4, which mitigated the lid-breaking risk most efficiently, over Scenario 1, which assumed the lid would not break.

There are many different types of discovery that can occur during a project. Most can be minimized with proper planning, but certainly not all. By definition, when we learn by doing and when time passes, we surface the need to refine our plan.

Every one of these changes affects the fundamental building blocks, our known work items. It may also affect our planned transformations, skills required, and priority and sequencing. For this reason, a truly flexible Agile process enforces the specification of the work in the manner described in the dependency tree scenarios above and provides tooling to quickly play out the new set of possible dependency trees (assembly lines) so flows can shift in an instant – and not wait until the sprint end.

By assuming the dependency tree problem is unsolvable in a systematic way, traditional Agile approaches do not put in the effort to think and plan far enough ahead to build one. Instead, they rely on heavy inter-sprint re-planning, with a view only until the end of the next sprint, when it has to happen all over again. For projects which need to make and meet clear commitments several sprints into the future, this approach is prone to surprises and failure.

Indeed, the Agile Codex approach and tooling cannot work if any of the principles around work item definition, sizing, tooling, or sequencing are not followed.

The Agile Codex Practice

Building Blocks
Planting the Tree

In order to track and record the deliverables through the release life cycle, let's define the building blocks, the objects that group each deliverable type, along with some high-level rules they conform to. All information and tracking of the work attach to these units. These units each have a single owner who is responsible for shepherding them through their life cycle.

There will be little in these blocks which vary in principle from standard Agile definitions, although where boundaries are drawn, and the abstraction level of a given hierarchy may vary. Those differences should not affect the truth of the principles and process.

You will see the reflections of a myriad of Agile tracking tools, all of which are valid systems for tracking the inputs to the Codex. My first development of the Codex, for example, took place in the context of Jira, and every building block detailed below conceptually aligns with the basic Jira objects and metadata.

These building blocks will be used to illustrate the flow of work through the release life cycle, from planning to execution to release.

© Michael McCormick 2021
M. McCormick, *The Agile Codex*, https://doi.org/10.1007/978-1-4842-7280-0_15

Planned Release

The Planned Release is simply the list of Epics in the release. This list is used during release planning to prioritize Epic sizing efforts for the release, and once the Epics are groomed, they are indicated in the list as committed to the release.

Owner: PM

- The list of Epics first considered, and then committed to for the Release.

Epic

An Epic groups User Stories and Bugs at the level of functional deliverable. The Epic provides a high-level list of requirements for a feature area, including UX user flows, vision statements, justifications, and narratives.

The feature requirements may be summarized with high-level Acceptance Criteria, often in terms of the user experience of the feature.

Owner: PM

- Groups User Stories by functional deliverable.

- Provides a high-level list of requirements for that feature area.

User Story

A User Story is the fundamental building block of software engineering work. It functions as the node in the dependency tree.

A User Story is owned by a single software engineer.

Acceptance Criteria

A User Story contains the Acceptance Criteria (AC) required to fulfill the work it represents as part of the Epic to which it belongs. The AC includes a definition of what the User Story delivers from a product standpoint, often written in terms of the experience of the user.

The AC also include the required behavior from an engineering standpoint, such as performance, testability, and design specifications and architectural foundations which support the user experience. The AC may also be further described by higher-resolution UX designs and flows relating to them.

Tasks

A User Story groups the software engineering Tasks required to deliver the functionality described in its AC. These tasks represent discrete items of work. Tasks are generally used to track discrete changes to the codebase, although they could also function as a to-do list for the engineer.

A User Story must contain at least one Task, and at least one Task must be associated with a proposed change to the codebase (e.g., a Pull Request in Git terms). If a User Story were to have no proposed changes to the codebase, it is not something that has a function in the dependency tree.

A Task should never be associated with more than one proposed change (progressive changes to a feature branch as the work is being done are still considered one change).

Dependencies

A User Story should indicate which proximal User Stories must be complete before it can be started and completed. These User Stories are dependencies and are children of the User Story.

A User Story will, in turn, be named as a child to any User Story which depends on it.

Try not to think of Stories as wrappers for other User Stories, from any standpoint beyond technical implementation. That is, if your User Story's AC cannot be fulfilled until another Story delivers an API, that story is your child. If you can fulfill your AC without it, it is not a child.

If your User Story's AC is so broad that it cannot be encapsulated wholly by specific tasks and PRs in the story, then your User Story is invalid and cannot function as a node in the dependency graph.

If your User Story has no function but to point to a set of child stories but has no code to be written for it, it is redundant to them and cannot be sized nor function as a node in the dependency graph and is therefore an invalid construction.

Adjacent Teams

Adjacent teams can use the User Story to represent their own work as it may relate to the User Story, such as QE test plans, UX designs, OPS deployment steps and DOC assets. Important: The User Story does NOT ever represent the tracking, assignment, or execution of the work of adjacent teams as this would break the principle of single ownership, which in turn makes it impossible to construct the dependency graph.

Story Points

A User Story indicates the amount of estimated effort required to deliver the software engineering work described in the AC. There are many competing theories with varying utility around how to point a User Story and whether or not points should be thought of as equaling days. I give this a big "they should," as the dependency tree tool I use relies on this approach.

A note on Effort versus Calendar time: Remember the function of the dependency graph is to minimize calendar delays by optimally sequencing work and dependencies across software engineers. If we include calendar time in our pointing, we are conflating the purpose of the node. Calendar time, by definition, represents the combination of effort time and delays. Delays should be minimized and dependencies should be identified as child nodes. By only pointing for effort, we can clearly see when the life of a User Story outgrows the effort being spent on it. If, in practice, we see calendar delays consistently growing over effort estimates, we have the signal we need to update our system to externalize those dependencies. More on that later.

Owner: One and only one DEV

- Encapsulates the
    - Acceptance Criteria (AC)
    - Tasks
- Same owner and executor as containing User Story
- Represent discrete units of work which never culminate in more than one pull request and may not be associated with a pull request at all
- At least one must be associated with a pull request
- Dependencies
- Effort level expressed in Story Points

Bug

A Bug is a type of User Story which expresses its AC in terms of a failing test case. Bugs may be associated with Epics if their delivery is a requirement for the delivery of the Epic. A Bug goes into the dependency tree just like a User Story.

Owner: One and only one DEV

- A type of User Story whose Acceptance Criteria are defined by a failing test case.

All Together

Together, these building blocks carry all the information we need to complete the full SDLC in any cadence, as long as they adhere to the rules of the Codex as defined above.

We can represent these building blocks as shown in Figure 15-1.

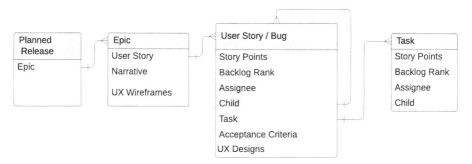

Figure 15-1. ERD of building blocks

Next, let's look at how these objects flow through the system.

Workflow

Tending the Tree

We have now defined the basic building blocks. The next step is to define how these building blocks move through the system, carrying data and transitioning states. We will revisit a couple of principles which inform how this happens:

- Clear ownership of work

- Clear inputs and input providers to each phase

- Clear transition criteria to transition work from one phase to the next

- Clear output and stakeholder approval

Each building block has a clearly defined owner as described in the previous chapter. Let us now walk through each building block and how they are shepherded through the planning, execution, and release phases.

Planning

We will go deep into the planning process that would happen in a multi-sprint release in order to touch on all the parts of planning that could be done. Changing resolution to short time frames and experimental projects change the planning / execution balance, which in turn changes the degree to which

M. McCormick, *The Agile Codex*, https://doi.org/10.1007/978-1-4842-7280-0_16

different steps of this process adhere (e.g., the amount of planning required between sprints versus before the release begins). Nothing, however, changes the principles and general flow. This starting point will give us the most thorough thought exercise.

We will discuss the inputs, iterations, outputs, and the subtleties around each step, as well as the artifacts they produce and how each team contributes to each phase. While the map and workflows may feel complex at first, keep in mind that each object has a single owner, and the knowledge and tracking of the objects through the workflow are delegated to that owner. In practice, each owner quickly learns their part in the whole orchestra. By dispersing intelligence and decision-making downward and enforcing the principles around how the objects are built and how they move, the project can quickly begin running itself, freeing managers to respond to signals emitted by the tracking tools and outside influences, rather than get lost in the minutiae of the day-to-day.

The phases of software delivery are broken down as follows:

- Release Planning
- Epic Grooming
- User Story Grooming
- Epic Commitment
- Execution
  - Tracking
  - Adjustments
- Releasing

Grooming is a key term used throughout this book. Grooming refers to the collaborative elaboration and refinement of requirements. In my practice, grooming can happen via face-to-face meetings as well as asynchronous discussions over messaging tools like Slack or shared documents via comments and revisions. Asynchronous discussions are very useful for giving participants time to think and research before giving feedback, and as they are written, there can be a permanent record of the discussion. In-person grooming is best for early brainstorming and communication of complex ideas and concepts for preliminary feedback or finalizing understanding.

Asynchronous discussions are very useful for giving participants time to think and research before giving feedback.

Grooming, as you will see below, is critical because of its function of including all stakeholders from beginning to end. What may seem like overhead at first glance becomes an incredibly efficient mechanism for transferring information and building cross-team relationships. The lack of surprises near the end of delivery pays for itself many times over, as do the established relationships and histories between the team members.

Release Planning is the process of grooming the initial, high-level set of requirements, broken into functional areas (called Epics) into enough detail that they can be prioritized into the next level of grooming.

Epic Grooming is the process of transforming Epic level requirements into more precise functional descriptions and acceptance criteria which are encapsulated in User Stories, along with the engineering designs required to fulfill the general design of the feature.

Story Grooming is the process of transforming Story level acceptance criteria resulting from the Epic into specific, actionable tasks which align with the product acceptance criteria as well as technical acceptance criteria.

Epic Commitment occurs when the sum quantity of work scoped for the Epic is confirmed to be within the resource budget available for the time period of the release. As such, a committed Epic is one the team has committed to complete by the end of the release.

Once an Epic is committed, *Execution* begins. Execution is the iterative process of doing, learning, and adjusting plans as new information arrives and external pressures modify direction.

When the *Release* is due, all committed Epics, modified as-needed through the software development cycle, are completed and delivered, and the software is packaged and deployed for distribution and customer access. Figure 16-1 captures this flow.

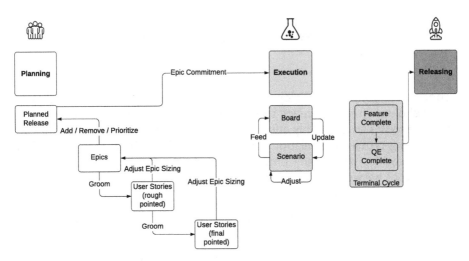

Figure 16-1. Phases of delivery

Release Planning

The PM owns the Planned Release, which holds the list of Epics to be considered for the release. Before Epics are committed for the release, they exist in this list as candidates, and the PM is responsible for providing adequate information to the DEV team to rough size the Epics.

Additionally, any release must be bounded by capacity – that is, how many software engineers are available to do the work in the time frame of the release. The EM is responsible for providing a budget of Story Points to the PM for guidance on release capacity. This can be bounded by the type of work the Story Points are available to do – for example, 50 points for web development and 200 points for API development.

The PM can use this guidance to set the grooming line of the Planned Release. Above this line indicates a desire, intention, and possibility of committing to the Epic for the release. Below the line means, given current understanding, an Epic is not going to fit (Figure 16-2).

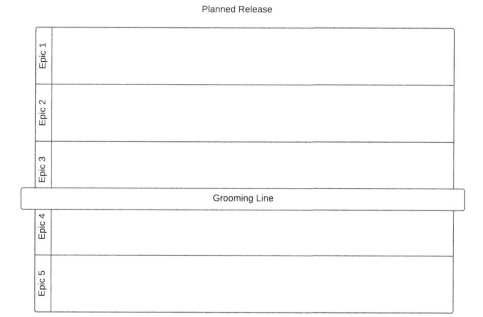

Figure 16-2. Planned Release and grooming line

Because even rough-sizing takes time, the PM also ranks them in order of rough-sizing priority. While Epics may be ranked in order of importance to consider for the release, they may also be bumped up or down based on the level of impact a given rough sizing would have on its rank on the list, implicitly bumping another Epic to be more important to rough size next (Figure 16-3).

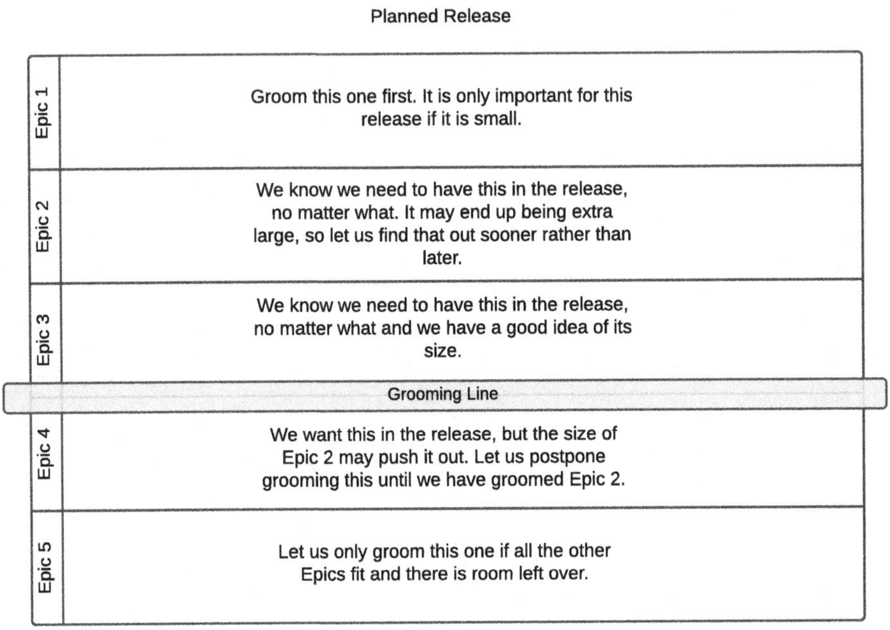

Planned Release

Epic 1	Groom this one first. It is only important for this release if it is small.
Epic 2	We know we need to have this in the release, no matter what. It may end up being extra large, so let us find that out sooner rather than later.
Epic 3	We know we need to have this in the release, no matter what and we have a good idea of its size.
	Grooming Line
Epic 4	We want this in the release, but the size of Epic 2 may push it out. Let us postpone grooming this until we have groomed Epic 2.
Epic 5	Let us only groom this one if all the other Epics fit and there is room left over.

Figure 16-3. Stack ranking the Epics

As owner of the Planned Release, the PM is responsible for bringing in all the relevant stakeholders required for rough sizing. In practice, this is usually a conversation with a domain expert from DEV and, if it is a customer-facing feature, UX. A dialog begins with these parties, teasing apart the information in the Epic, brainstorming the broad engineering tasks that will be required, and looking for unexpected complexity.

Once the DEV representatives are comfortable with the information they have, they give it a rough size. On my teams, we follow this pattern:

```
XS =  8-24 pts (1-3 person weeks)
S  = 24-48 pts (3-6 person weeks)
M  = 48-96 pts (6-12 person weeks)
L  = 96-192 pts (12-24 person weeks)
XL = 192-384 pts (24-48 person weeks)
```

Note that the larger the Epic, the greater the range in rough size. This reflects both the amount of work and uncertainty. During rough-sizing discussions, large initial sizing can drive toward clarity and simplification of the Epic, encouraging a lean mind-set and a quality first pass at the Epic AC. Figure 16-4 depicts the narrowing of uncertainty as estimates are iteratively refined.

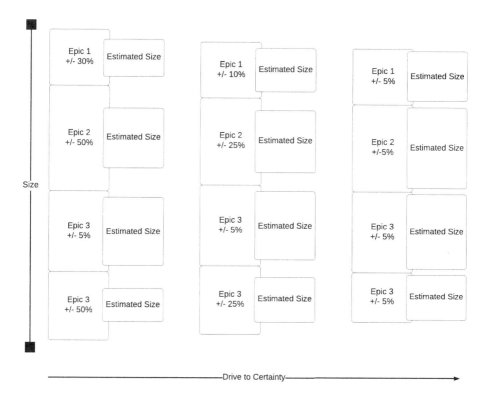

Figure 16-4. Iterative grooming drives down uncertainty in scope of work

It usually makes sense to rough size an Epic or two below the grooming line as these may be considered later as stretch goals on the chance that during the execution phase, extra engineering time becomes available.

Summarizing the Release Planning phase (see Figure 16-5):

- Owner: PM
- Inputs:
  - Story Point budget from EM
  - Candidate Epics, Ranked
- Transition Criteria:
  - PM, EM, DEV discuss and refine in order
  - Re-ranking may occur as a result of discussions
- Outputs:
  - Ranked list of rough-sized Epics above and slightly below the grooming line

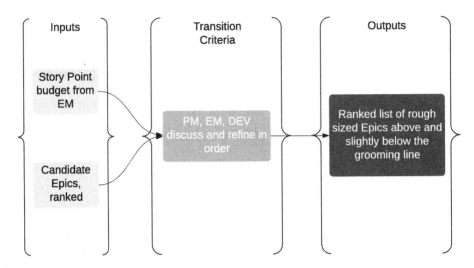

Figure 16-5. Release Planning phase

Epic Grooming

Once the Epics above the grooming line (and possibly a few below) have been rough sized, it means we know which ones are worth investing time into to bring them to a higher resolution of sizing certainty. This is the Epic Grooming phase.

During rough-sizing, the Epic was refined to the point at which its UX and AC were understood enough to be rough-sizable. As the owner of the Epic, the PM is now responsible for bringing the Epic grooming team together.

The Epic grooming team involves the PM and one or more representatives from UX (if applicable to the Epic), DEV, QE, OPS, and DOC. It is the responsibility of this team to continue the refinement of the Epic AC to the point at which User Stories can be constructed. These User Stories must have enough detail in them to be rough point-able by DEV. PM and DEV work together to generate these User Stories and refine their AC to a rough-point-able state.

While User Stories do not need to be fully specified with software engineering tasks at this point, they must be structured and intended to conform to the Agile Codex principle of being a "discrete, single-owner, low-risk, rapidly deliverable, reviewable, and sequenceable unit conforming to participate as an eligible node in the project's full acyclic dependency tree" once the final grooming is done.

UX, QE, OPS, and DOC primarily play the role of interface to their areas of concern, questioning edge cases, bringing up inconsistencies they may see, and any engineering challenges such as testability (QE) or builds and environments (OPS). The presence of these teams provides three essential functions:

- Information: Critical extra input toward DEV and PM understanding and specifying the requirements beyond just the focused engineering scope of the work

- Familiarity: A seat at the table from the beginning, so downstream, detailed User Story Grooming they are also involved in does not happen context-free

- Collaboration: A voice in the work that is coming their way and face time with their teammates

Once the Epic is full of its rough pointed Stories, the sum total size replaces the rough size from the initial release planning phase. As this clarity happens, the ranking of Epics in the Planned Release may continue to shift, informing the consequent priority of the next Epics to groom.

Summarizing the Epic Grooming phase (see Figure 16-6):

- Owner: PM
- Inputs:
    - UX, DEV, QE, OPS, DOC
- Transition Criteria:
    - Epic grooming team discuss and refine
    - PM & DEV create User Stories which are clear enough to be rough pointed by DEV
- Outputs:
    - Sign-off from the Epic grooming team
    - An Epic whose size is now the sum of the rough pointed User Stories it contains
    - A possible re-ranking of Epics in the Planned Release

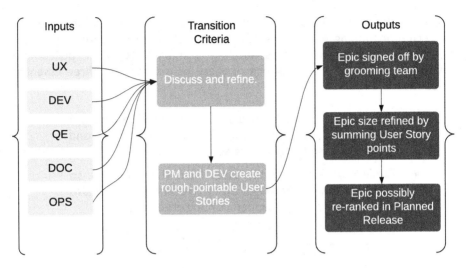

Figure 16-6. Epic Grooming phase

User Story Grooming

This next phase transforms the rough pointed User Stories into those final pointed, fully groomed units of work conforming to the Agile Codex core principle:

Define work in discrete, single-owner, low-risk, rapidly deliverable, reviewable, and sequenceable units conforming to participate as an eligible node in the project's full acyclic dependency tree.

And continues to adhere to the state change principles:

- Clear contract between parties moving work from one state to another
- Clear inputs and input providers to each state
- Clear output and stakeholder approval to transition state

The User Story is owned by one DEV. This DEV is responsible for assembling the User Story Grooming team. This is most often, and logically, the same team that groomed the parent Epic.

The primary function of the DEV at this point is to specify the software engineering Tasks which are required to be performed to satisfy the AC of the User Story. This usually leads to more discussions and revisions as the UX moves from high-level wire frame to specific page designs, flows, and validations at the User Story level. These revisions are reflected in updated and finalized AC, which include both PM AC, usually expressed in user-centric language: "As a user..." and DEV AC, which point to specific engineering requirements.

The DEV proposes the final AC and Tasks to the grooming team, which then has the responsibility to understand their part in delivering the work and to sign-off and commit to that understanding. This sign-off can be thought of as a statement of sorts: "I, QE, understand how to test this User Story's AC" and "I, OPS, know how I will be deploying this work to each environment," and "I, DOC, know how I will describe this feature to the end users." If, at any point during the grooming there are questions or concerns from these adjacent teams, they must be brought to bear, and AC and Tasks updated to reflect any revisions they drive.

DEV must also indicate which User Stories are children of this User Story, meaning which User Stories must happen before work on this User Story can be done.[1]

Once every member of the grooming team signs off, the User Story is final pointed by DEV and considered ready for work.

Summarizing the Story Grooming phase (see Figure 16-7):

- Owner: DEV
- Inputs:
  - UX, PM, QE, OPS, DOC
- Transition Criteria:
  - User Story Grooming team discuss and refine
  - AC of User Story are refined, including clarifying UX, product AC, and adding any engineering-specific AC required to deliver the work
  - DEV creates engineering Tasks which correspond to fulfilling the AC of the User Story
  - DEV assigns final points
  - DEV defines dependencies as parent / child User Story relationship
- Outputs:
  - Sign-off from the User Story Grooming team

---

[1] It is possible to specify a parent as well, but it is easier to just think of children. If any given User Story has a parent, it will get linked as a child when the parent is groomed.

- An Agile Codex-conforming node in the dependency tree ready for execution

- An Epic whose size is finalized as the sum of all the final pointed User Stories it contains

- A possible re-ranking of Epics in the Planned Release

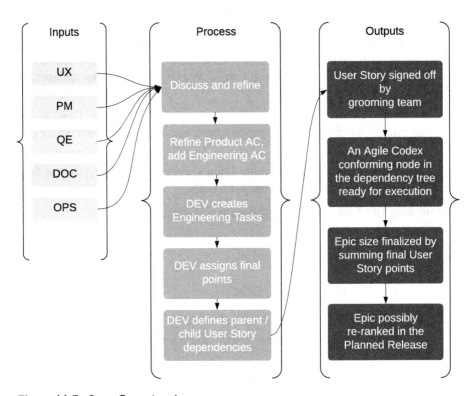

Figure 16-7. Story Grooming phase

Epic Commitment

Once all the User Stories in the Epic are signed-off, their final points are summed, and the Epic size is also finalized. The Epic may at any point then be committed to the release based on the continued evaluation of priority, size, and budget. The PM updates the Planned Release list to indicate that the Epic is now committed (Figure 16-8).

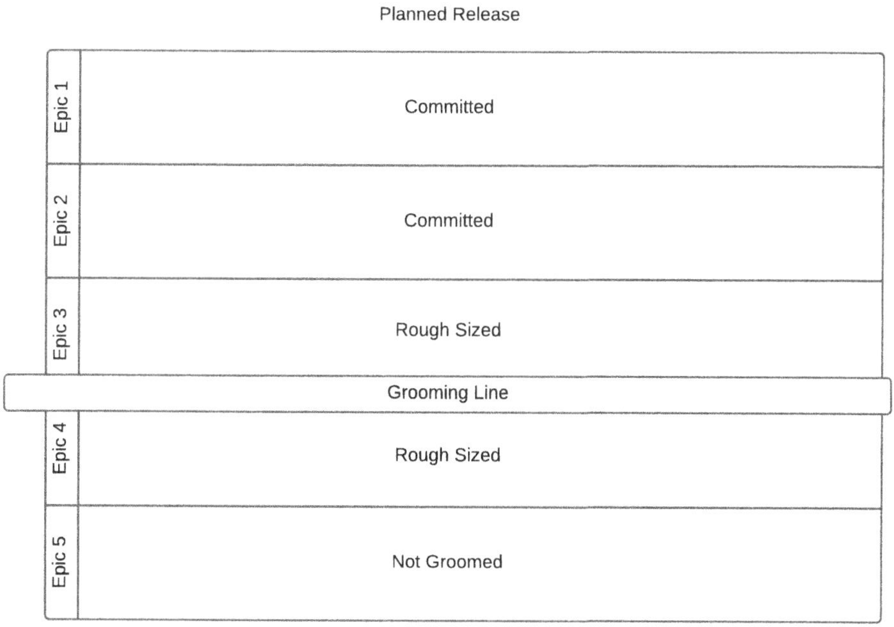

Planned Release

Epic 1	Committed
Epic 2	Committed
Epic 3	Rough Sized
Grooming Line	
Epic 4	Rough Sized
Epic 5	Not Groomed

Figure 16-8. Epic Commitment as reflected in the Planned Release

Execution
Setting Up the Tree

Now it is time to take our conforming User Stories and figure out which of the many possible dependency trees we should plan and execute on.

There are two variables moving at the same time:

- Assignee (imagine this as the "Tool" from our saltshaker example)

- Sequence – the order in which any non-dependent User Stories would be executed (recall the thread and perforate tasks, from the saltshaker example, which could happen in either order)

And two invariants:

- Dependency – what must happen before another thing

- Size – the amount of effort required to complete the task

Because of the interdependence of these inputs, it is easiest to simply assert a starting point for the two variables we can control, visualize the consequences, and then make adjustments to those inputs interactively.

To do this visualization, we need a tool which will allow us to link User Stories as dependencies. We also need a tool which will represent these dependencies, assigned to a user, being executed over time, with no two tasks being performed simultaneously by the same user. For the latter, we need a very smart Gantt chart whose focus is *projection*, not proscription.

Never fear! I wrote such a Gantt chart generator using Google Sheets, which is accessible on my website, michaelmccormick.com.

The inputs are each User Story with

- All child User Stories
- Story Points
- Assignee
- Sequence the assignee will work on the User Story

The output is a visualization which shows when each item will start, how long it will take to complete, and who will work on it. The dependency formulas in the sheet will ensure that no parent can start before all its children are complete.

Below is a stylized diagram illustrating the essentials. Please refer to the spreadsheet for detailed instructions around practical use.

Figure 16-9 shows the mapping of Story Points to days of effort in the Gantt.

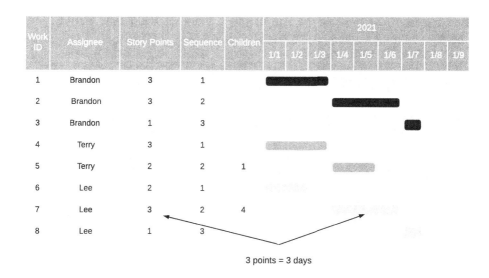

Figure 16-9. Story Points as days in the Gantt

Figure 16-10 reflects the sequencing of work for each DEV.

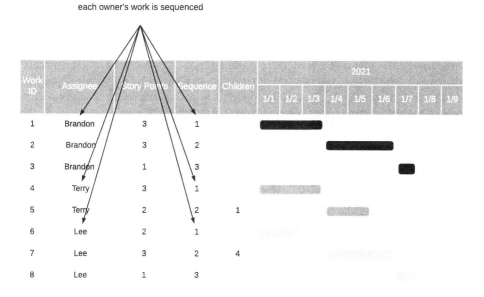

Figure 16-10. Sequence of work for each User Story owner in the Gantt

And Figure 16-11 depicts the use of the Children attribute to identify and enforce required sequencing of work.

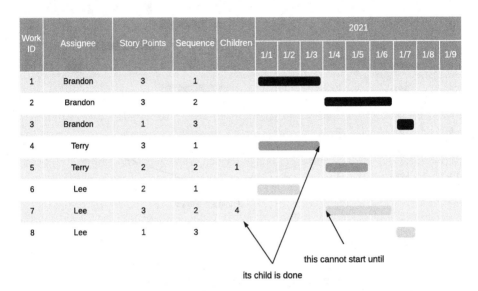

Work ID	Assignee	Story Points	Sequence	Children	2021								
					1/1	1/2	1/3	1/4	1/5	1/6	1/7	1/8	1/9
1	Brandon	3	1										
2	Brandon	3	2										
3	Brandon	1	3										
4	Terry	3	1										
5	Terry	2	2	1									
6	Lee	2	1										
7	Lee	3	2	4									
8	Lee	1	3										

this cannot start until

its child is done

Figure 16-11. Child attribute enforcing sequencing of User Stories in the Gantt

Here is how it works.

First, we visually inspect the chart for gaps. Recall that a gap represents an engineer who is idle while waiting for a dependent User Story to be completed. When we see the gap, we can adjust the plan to close it by either shuffling the assignment of the User Stories or by changing the sequence an assignee is working on their User Stories as shown in Figure 16-12.

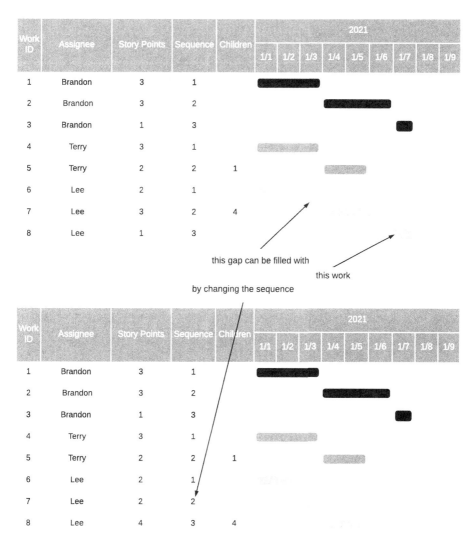

Figure 16-12. Changing the sequence of work to close a gap

We can also project the work all the way to the final day the final task will be completed. If we see any assignees ending after other assignees, we can rebalance work between them (Figure 16-13).

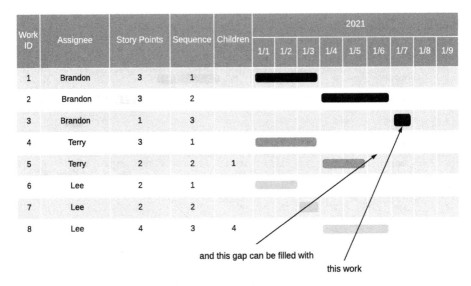

Figure 16-13. Changing the assignee of work to close a gap

And, of course, if we see that we are completing work after the release should be complete, we know that we are over-committed and we can adjust scope by removing User Stories from the release, or by cutting scope within User Stories (Figure 16-14).

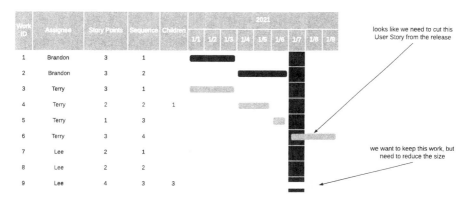

Figure 16-14. Changing the scope of work, and excluding work to deliver to a release commitment date

If we need to make further adjustments, we can tune the ratio more directly by using the velocity modifier input parameter at the top of the sheet, which applies to all developers equally, or we can specifically indicate availability and even days off work for a given person.

The Board

Now our assembly line is set up and we are ready to start work. Work is tracked on a traditional Agile board with the User Stories moving through several distinct phases. Keep in mind that this wall is an example of a flow and not the only possible form such could take. The most important thing to understand is the phases the work goes through, and the principle of clear ownership when moving from phase to phase.

The board contains both types of work, User Stories and Bugs. The principal difference between the two in the flow described below is that bugs do not generally need to be groomed or signed-off.

Also recall that the work on the wall is owned by one DEV and only one DEV throughout all the phases.

Each phase is visually represented as a column on the wall, and the flow to closure is left to right (Figure 16-15).

Needs Sign-Off	Signed Off	Development	Fix Required	Test	PM / UX Review	Closed

Figure 16-15. Phases of User Stories on the board

Needs Sign-Off

Sometimes a User Story will come into existence during the Execution phase. These must be groomed and signed off as any other User Story would. This column signifies that the grooming team must be engaged and sign-off obtained before beginning work. When sign-off is approved, DEV moves the User Story to the next phase.

Signed Off

Any User Story that is signed off and ready for work, but not yet started, lives in this column. Once a DEV begins work, DEV moves the User Story to the next phase.

In Progress

This column reflects the User Stories which are currently being worked on. During this phase, each Task is executed until all Tasks are complete.

Any discovery during this phase, such as questions about a nuance around the AC, or confirmation on a UX detail which was not spelled out, happen as needed and informally. If something is discovered which would increase the scope of the User Story, either points can be adjusted in-place, or a new User Story can be constructed as a Parent, to be executed when the User Story in progress is complete. Adjustments to AC must be documented in the User Story both to inform the Grooming Team, as well as to serve as the source-of-record of what is being delivered. The more capable a team becomes in planning, the smaller the requirements escape one would expect to see.

Some Tasks will involve changes to the code repository. Each Task is by definition discrete (as they are checked in independently) and as a consequence of the User Story being constrained in size, small in scope, and generally simple and quick to review for approval to check in. Thus, the principle of keeping work small and its life cycle on the wall short also leads to more frequent, lower-risk, and efficiently reviewable deliveries of code.

When all Tasks are complete, DEV moves the User Story to the QE phase.

Fix Needed

As mentioned above, this phase signifies there is now a Child work item which must be addressed before this User Story can be passed through the QE phase. When the owning DEV delivers all the Child work, the DEV then moves this back to the QE phase.

QE

During the QE phase, the User Story is tested. Between sign-off and this phase, QE will have created a test plan to verify the AC. Only QE work which needs to be done to approve the User Story AC blocks the User Story from moving from this phase. Asynchronous QE work, such as automation tasks and integration testing, are not generally blocking or specifically targeted at verifying the specific ACs of the User Story, so they can happen out-of-band of the User Story workflow.

If any AC fails testing, QE creates a Bug as a Child of the User Story, moves the User Story to the Fix Needed column, and the Bug then enters the Workflow in the Signed-Off column (Bugs do not generally need grooming). As a Child, the Bug indicates that it must be completed before the Parent is considered complete, and the dependency tree is enforced during any replanning. Once the Bug is closed, the DEV can move the User Story from Fix Needed and QE once again is done against the User Story AC.

If any questions arise around ambiguity in the AC or interpretations made by DEV during the implementation work, they are resolved with the grooming team. Changes resulting from those discussions can either be reflected by a new User Story (which can be tagged in order to audit and evaluate requirements escape over time) or a Bug. If the change should block completion of the original User Story, the new work would be created as a Child and worked as described above. If the change would not block completion, it would not be created as a Child.

If no issues are found and all tests of the AC pass, the QE moves the User Story to PM / UX / DOC Review.

PM / UX

There is more to verify in a User Story than merely the core functionality at the level of QE. Aligning with the principle of many quality gates, this last phase is where the requirement inputs of delivery verify that their understanding of what they signed-off on was met. The PM owns the coordination of this verification, involving UX if applicable.

As with the QE phase, if anything is amiss, an evaluation is made as to whether or not it was requirements escape or implementation error, and whether or not the miss is blocking. The same remediation steps occur as in the QE phase (new User Story or Bug, Child or independent, move to Fix Needed).

When all verification is complete, the work is moved by PM to Closed.

Closed

Work in this phase is complete and this phase is final and immutable. No work leaves this phase. Anything discovered after the fact which relates to the work must be a new work item.

Once work is closed, and only when work is closed, can the parent of the work also be closed.

A .pdf outlining this entire flow is also available on michaelmccormick.com.

We use this handy reference to keep the workflow clear, from Epic to User Story delivery. The leftmost column indicates the team, and the top row indicates the object and phase. The intersection of the two gives a direct instruction on the role of that team representative with respect to the object as it enters and exits the phase.

As you can see, this allows the intelligence and coordination around an inherently complex process to be delegated out into far simpler, and eventually skillful habits for each team representative.

External Dependencies

The work on the board is directly owned only by DEV. Depending on the organization structure, and the nature of a given project, there may be other teams upon which the delivery of any given collection of work depends. These are effectively children which live outside of the team and board.

Good tooling and common practices between teams allow linking a node on one team's board to a node on another team's board, effectively linking the Gantt projections by the date that the linked child is scheduled for delivery.

In circumstances where this level of coordination is not possible, it is the responsibility of the DEV owner of the work to interface with the dependency and coordinate delivery, informing project management of estimated delivery date. The delegation of this ownership to the DEV distributes responsibility throughout the system and also aligns with the principle of collaboration and building cross-team relationships from the ground up.

One trick we have used on my teams is to create a proxy User Story as a child to whatever dependent node we have in our tree, placing it on the Gantt according to the projected delivery date. Figure 16-16 shows how this looks.

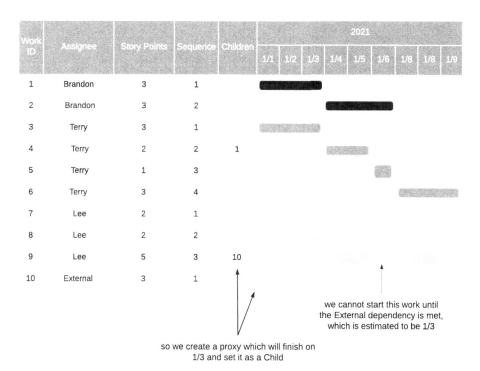

Work ID	Assignee	Story Points	Sequence	Children	2021								
					1/1	1/2	1/3	1/4	1/5	1/6	1/8	1/8	1/9
1	Brandon	3	1										
2	Brandon	3	2										
3	Terry	3	1										
4	Terry	2	2	1									
5	Terry	1	3										
6	Terry	3	4										
7	Lee	2	1										
8	Lee	2	2										
9	Lee	5	3	10									
10	External	3	1										

we cannot start this work until the External dependency is met, which is estimated to be 1/3

so we create a proxy which will finish on 1/3 and set it as a Child

Figure 16-16. Using a proxy User Story to represent the estimated delivery of an external dependency

There can also be dependencies the other way; the reverse method can be used. The dependent team can simply look at the Gantt chart and know the ETA of whatever node they depend on.

Even QE, within the team, can do this trick, as the Gantt very specifically shows when development work on a User Story is estimated to be complete, and thus ready for shifting to the QE phase (Figure 16-17).

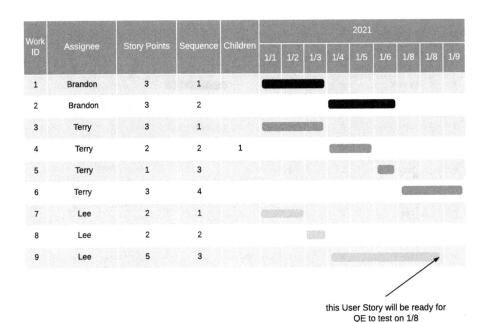

Figure 16-17. How dependent external teams can use the Gantt to know when work will be delivered

The Sprint or the Kanban

Note that nothing about sprints or Kanban has been mentioned with respect to the execution phase. This is intentional, as the flow and planning process are, in principle, no different.

The intention of these different styles is largely to set a cadence for certain ceremonies, specifically when to plan and when to measure.

Traditionally, sprints are designed to plan, execute, and measure at two-to-four-week intervals. These date boundaries can also be leveraged to communicate and track dependencies. Thus, sprint approaches are more often used in project-based work with cross-team dependencies.

In contrast, Kanban tends to distribute planning and execution evenly throughout the entire delivery, even to the point of eschewing the idea of a given delivery date at all. Kanban, as such, tends to be used on small, independent teams, where work is less predictable and commitment dates are less business-impacting at a project level. Kanban can flex all the way to systems which have no single delivery at all, such as on-demand ticketing in an IT department.

Using the Agile Codex method renders sprint measure intervals redundant, as it allows for instant prediction all the way to project end at any time, and trends toward and away a set point can be identified every moment the dependency tree changes, as work arrives, begins, and completes.

Adjusting

By following the workflow rules above, the carefully constructed dependency tree maintains its integrity throughout the flex of a project. So long as the tree maintains its integrity, and the tracking system reflects it accurately, the Gantt will instantly surface any gaps that appear in the flow, or changes to the cumulative time remaining caused by things such as requirements escape, code quality variance, unexpected changes to external dependency delivery dates, and mis-estimated Story Points.

It is a simple matter at that point to adjust the assignments and sequencing to close gaps and minimize calendar time, exactly as was done at project start.

If, after resequencing, the final delivery date has still moved to the right, adjustments can be made, and external dependents notified. Of course, if it moves in, more work can be added.

Releasing

The Releasing phase is where feature work on the product winds down, final testing is completed, and the product is packaged for delivery.

Feature Complete

Using the Agile Codex approach, QE is able to do functional testing as work is delivered. In any project, there is a lag time from when a User Story is complete and quality review is complete. Similarly, in a release as a whole, there is also a lag time where all the pieces have come together, QE finishes any asynchronous work, and full integration testing of the end-to-end product becomes possible.

It is useful to set a Feature Complete date early enough before the packaging phase to allow time for this asynchronous QE work to complete, and for any release-blocking bugs uncovered during that work to also be fixed and verified using the established workflow (see Figure 16-18).

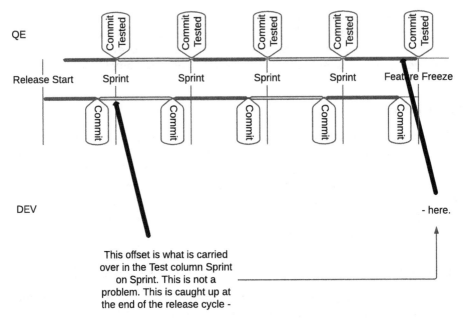

Figure 16-18. Accounting for the offset between User Story delivery from DEV and testing by QE through the sprint and release cycles

As an Agile project manager, one must be very careful during this time to avoid the temptation to stop testing in order to meet a "zero bug" metric, or to set such an arbitrary and unrealistic standard for a release to be accepted. In reality, testing can have a very long tail. Strong QE planning involves testing the highest-risk areas first, before Feature Freeze, in order to minimize the quantity of high-severity bugs found after Feature Freeze.

QE Complete

Once the QE work is complete and all release-blocking bugs have been fixed and verified, the Release is ready to be packaged for delivery.

The Terminal Sprint

Depending on how long QE needs to complete the asynchronous testing work, and DEV needs to fix and deliver issues found, one may choose a single sprint or perhaps more. The feature commit date established during the planning process should account for this time. For our purposes in this book, we will talk about this final QE phase as something which fits in a single, terminal sprint, for simplicity. This terminal sprint begins with Feature Complete (all feature User Stories delivered) and ends with QE Complete.

As DEV is winding down feature work, and only responding to bugs raised during final testing, they generally have extra time. This is the perfect time to begin planning the next release.

Metrics

Measure Matters

In order to analyze, report, and adjust our processes, we need to measure them. These analyses allow us to better predict each cycle, report on how well we executed according to plan, how well we planned to begin with, and how our deviations from plan impacted our delivery, both positive and negative.

Whenever we talk about metrics, we must acknowledge that there is never a perfect blending of map to territory. Software developers will always optimize their planning and execution to the information they have, and that planning and execution may not be perfectly captured in the methods they are provided to record the work they are doing.

When faced with decisions around doing versus recording, if there is any friction between the two, two things will result. First, some things will simply not be recorded, and some of these things would truly be important to know. Second, the things which are recorded may not represent the work with high fidelity, if the metrics themselves do not measure the important or even relevant aspects of the work.

This disconnect causes noise in the system at best, and breaks the integrity of the Codex at worst. As such, it is critical to always monitor the work being done against the value of the way it is recorded. This disconnect, more importantly, is a sign that the system and processes need to be improved.

© Michael McCormick 2021
M. McCormick, *The Agile Codex*, https://doi.org/10.1007/978-1-4842-7280-0_17

When individuals are relied upon to send signals and there are no systemic guardrails around how and when these signals are acknowledged and acted upon, optimized coordination breaks down.

In the absence of a useful process, a shadow organization organically arises out of the necessities of individuals. Everyone self-optimizes the process from their perspective, playing out their own idiomatic interpretation of what they believe needs to be done, which is likely to be materially different from the person sitting next to them.

When information is siloed and semantics and meaning are no longer shared, there is no common philosophy or standard for resolving ambiguity. When facing unfamiliar situations, individual judgments vary. Unaware of and unable to measure the activity of the shadow organization, the project suffers as the manager is forced to make decisions with incomplete and non-transferable data emanating from each local decider.

Figure 17-1 depicts the intersection between what I, the developer, do, what I record I am doing, and what you, the project manager, need in order to make good planning decisions.

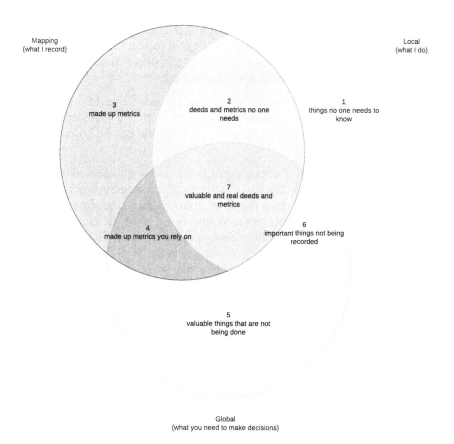

Mapping
(what I record)

Local
(what I do)

3
made up metrics

2
deeds and metrics no one needs

1
things no one needs to know

7
valuable and real deeds and metrics

4
made up metrics you rely on

6
important things not being recorded

5
valuable things that are not being done

Global
(what you need to make decisions)

Figure 17-1. The intersections of deed, recording, and deciding

It is an incredibly useful exercise to show this diagram to a team, and ask them to fill in each area with real world examples from their projects. It helps put context and safety around process critiques coming from the team, as well as giving the team an idea of how their local information is a critical part of the global decision-making process.

Predicting

Most Agile methodologies emphasize team velocity as a gold-standard metric. Velocity is measured between two points in time. Sprint boundaries are logical points in time, while Kanban, being boundaryless, can be measured between any two points, so long as history at those points is being tracked.

This velocity is used to predict the rate at which the next set of work will be executed. Differences in velocity from one cycle to the next are interpreted as a signal that something is going wrong, and the plus / minus on any future estimates grows or shrinks based on that stability.

Because the Agile Codex predicts the entire project's execution order and timing at any point in time, measuring velocity is similar to Kanban. Every snapshot of the dependency tree at each point in time can be compared with any prior point in time.

But velocity as a measure of effort spent is a shallow number which tells us little about customer value delivered without also understanding what that time was spent doing. Nor does it tell us anything about how we performed with respect to risk to the business. Simply doing work does not mean we met our deadlines or spent our time doing the right work. Change is not bad, but when change impacts velocity and velocity is *the* first-class metric, teams can be incentivized to hit commitments even while knowing they are the wrong things to be doing. Bad news is hidden, to be revealed later, when it will be more expensive to remedy.

Analyzing

As we have seen, there are two significant indicators that the Gantt view gives us: calendar time and effort time. Also, as we have seen, the difference between the two can tell us how efficiently we have distributed and ordered the work at any point in time, but it cannot tell us how efficiently we have planned at a project level or executed at an individual level.

Recall the example of the breakable lid during the perforation step: the scenario optimizing for that would not have appeared optimized compared with the zero-risk scenario until after the project completed and a lid broke.

Looking back at our lid-breaking scenario versus the idealistic scenario, we can derive the following key metrics: customer value delivered (total work done including filling in gaps with opportunistic work) and unexpected calendar shift (missing or beating a deadline commitment). Figure 17-2 charts this.

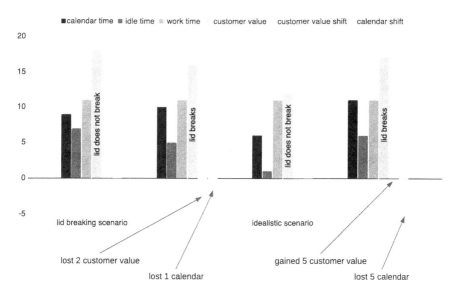

Figure 17-2. The subtle trade-offs of discovery and commitment

In the lid-breaking scenario, if the lid were to break, we risk a smaller calendar day loss of 1 versus 5. We also see a smaller shift in the sum of Work plus Idle time of -2 versus +5.

The important information these metrics carry is that it is not a zero-sum game. If we accept that Story Points are a proxy for customer value,[1] we can see that trade-offs are implicitly made around deadline misses and customer value. In some cases, it may be all right to miss a calendar date by five when the amount of extra work you were able to deliver along with that miss was also five. It may, on the other hand, be so important to hit a calendar date that it is worth minimizing the potential miss to one at the cost of actually losing two units of work overall.

In other words, some customers may be willing to accept a miss of five days on a commitment when they also understand that five more units of value were also delivered. Some may not.

Conveying these nuances both before and after the fact allows all levels of the business to have transparency and come to agreement on what is acceptable risk and what is not, and what trade-offs can mitigate others, as soon as possible and at any time.

---

[1] Obviously, a simplification, as much customer value is represented in aggregate as an Epic.

In cases where we did not realize there was a risk, and something goes wrong, we can go back in time and evaluate the cost of the risk directly. In our example, we can show that, indeed, we lost five calendar days, yet we gained more idle time – more gaps – which we were able to fill with work providing customer value. We can do this to the day.

How do we go back in time? Every snapshot of the dependency tree at any given point in time has all the necessary inputs to generate all the other possible trees! All we need to do is keep a historical record of the tree every time we generate it. Any number of scenarios before and after can be compared and a chart such as the one above can be generated, allowing everyone to understand how the project was affected by changes both positively and negatively.

In doing so, we can replace anecdotes with data, and simplified rubrics with nuance. All parties can acknowledge, confirm and adjust which of these axes they want to optimize for as planning and execution continue forward.

Adjusting

Recall that planning is simply the optimized strategy for risk minimization, where risk can be optimized toward calendar or total work, or some combination of the two, and risk includes today risk and tomorrow risk.

To understand how efficiently we have planned, after the fact, we need to track three axes:

- Requirements escape
- Effort time estimated versus effort time spent
- Total effort time versus calendar time for the entirety of the release

Requirements escape, also sometimes called scope creep, or discovered scope, is reflected in the additive changes to User Story AC which have a material impact on the effort time, which itself can be tracked by the emergence of child User Stories during acceptance testing by QE and PM / UX as per the example Agile Codex board flow.

Effort time *estimated* versus effort time *spent* simply reflects the variance between what time an individual expected to be working on an item compared with how much time they did spend, all other things being equal. This can be tracked by watching the deviation of calendar time from effort time for any given work item. Work items which stay on the board longer than their effort time indicate a possible issue.

Work items which stay on the board longer than their effort time indicate a possible issue.

Because the Agile Codex method allows us to dynamically replan the assembly line at any time, this inexpensive replanning and flexible retooling process is not a clear signal that something went wrong, but merely that something changed. The key is to simply identify both specific things which changed and patterns of change. By having a historical record of all possible trees at any given time, requirements escape numbers and effort time drifts, patterns of planning failure and effort-estimate failure (accounting for today risk) can be teased out from external influences (absorbing tomorrow risk as it moves into the present).

Once we identify patterns, we can modify the emphasis we place on any given area moving forward and again measure the difference it makes at any given point in time.

Opportunistic and Non-Epic Work

No matter how well work is planned, sequenced, and allocated, there will still be occasional gaps. This is the perfect place to put opportunistic work. Most products have a backlog of technical debt and bugs which may not fit into an intentional planning of a release. By their nature, they are generally free-standing (no dependencies) and relatively small.

Because they are not committed, they can be swapped in and out and moved to any spot during the release that makes sense, and because they fit in the gaps between committed work, they do not impact delivery of the committed work (Figure 17-3).

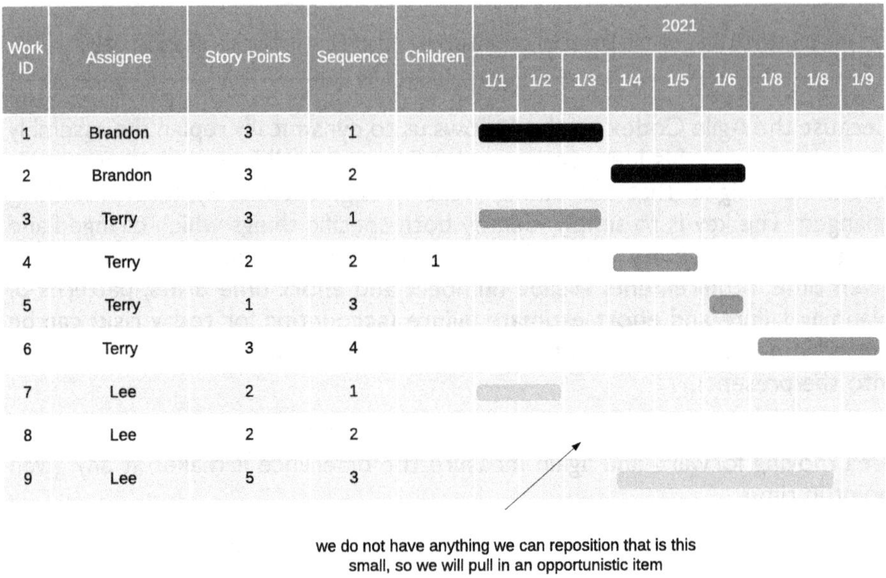

Work ID	Assignee	Story Points	Sequence	Children	2021								
					1/1	1/2	1/3	1/4	1/5	1/6	1/8	1/8	1/9
1	Brandon	3	1		███████								
2	Brandon	3	2					████████					
3	Terry	3	1			██████							
4	Terry	2	2	1				█████					
5	Terry	1	3							██			
6	Terry	3	4									███████	
7	Lee	2	1		████								
8	Lee	2	2										
9	Lee	5	3						█████████				

we do not have anything we can reposition that is this small, so we will pull in an opportunistic item

Figure 17-3. Inserting opportunistic work

Opportunistic gaps can be very good news for customers as they present opportunities to deliver unexpected value. They can also be good news internally, as they provide opportunities to pay down tech debt and reduce friction on the development and maintenance of the product into the future.

Multi-release Epics

Epics which cover the delivery of a multi-part feature, or a large feature which is not to be exposed to users until the entirety of the code is complete can simply be cut into two separate Epics. The feature work can be planned and delivered as usual in each release, with the only difference being the public exposure of the feature is hidden behind a feature flag.

Planning for a multi-release Epic is best done as a whole. Planning should happen to the level of User Story rough pointing until the sum total of points indicates the Epic is sized correctly for the Planned Release as a whole. Once that clarity is obtained, there is a decreasing return on investment of planning time toward further User Story level grooming. Having enough thought put into the Epic and a trailing handful of User Stories that do not get committed offers the opportunity to pull in and deliver extra work if the opportunity arises. As discussed earlier, things change and learning happens, so planning too far forward can end up wasting time. This is a judgment that an experienced manager can make once proximal clarity is achieved through planning the work in temporal order, gaining clarity iteratively.

Teaching the Teams

Simply Complex

Understandably, nearly all Agile approaches are designed with the implicit assumption that dependency management is hard, and, in fact, too expensive to manage, plan for, or predict. As a consequence, Agile processes which grudgingly acknowledge dependencies work very hard to remove them, minimize them, or pretend that they do not exist.

Often, backlogs are dependency trees compressed and stacked in a linear order. Or teams are resourced to make developers as fungible as possible. In the case of sprints, work is defined with two-week sprint boundary blinders on. For Kanban, work is defined as a result of immediately preceding work. Both operate at some level on the faith that dependencies take care of themselves, as it is "obvious" that nothing can be built on top of a thing which has not already been built.

When the inevitable questions come as to when a thing will be delivered, the clarity of answer fades rapidly beyond the sprint and Kanban time frames of two weeks or a preceding work item or two. What is going to be delivered is fairly clear in the short term, so long as it is a thing that can be defined into

M. McCormick, *The Agile Codex*, https://doi.org/10.1007/978-1-4842-7280-0_18

that time frame. Once the time frame expands into the future, both the *what* and the *when* fade. The argument of Agile is that because dependency management is hard, and plans change, this is the best we can do. It is not worth planning for the future: we do not know what we are doing next week, but that is good, because what we are doing next week is going to change anyway.

As a consequence, processes and tools which do acknowledge dependencies, and more, which spend time planning for and tracking them, carry a non-Agile stigma. Gantt charts, as primary and static tools of waterfall, receive strong approbation. Having specialized resources for each type of work a project needs, is considered a risk and weakness. Cross-team and cross-functional dependencies are even broader forms of this weakness to be avoided.

In this model, developers and product managers are not taught or encouraged to think of their work in terms of dependencies, leading to feature bleed across multiple work items, disconnected from the order a design might be ideally constructed, with overlapping and potentially overwriting and refactoring work delivered by different developers at different stages of the product's development.

It is no surprise that an Agile model that introduces a dependency tree as its atomic construct would cause confusion to the point of shouts of Agile blasphemy.

From Agile to Agile Codex

In my experience, the two primary objections can be boiled down to the following:

- A dependency tree for an entire project is too hard for any one person to build.

- That level of planning will take a lot of meetings and time, slowing us down.

On the surface, these are legitimate concerns. In response to the first, I point to the flow diagram and ask each team representative "where in your row here is your role unclear?" The point being that indeed, no one does need to build the entire dependency tree. The tree builds itself as each person in each role does their part. If the answer is "yes, it is unclear," then I know how I need to clarify the expression of that role (indeed, this is how these roles have grown into their current shape).

The second concern has several layers and assumptions built into it.

First, human nature being what it is, we tend to avoid things that are hard. Planning – the act of imagining all the ways things could be constructed, used, and go wrong in the process – is a lot of work. The best planners are the best worriers as well, always looking around corners and anticipating disaster. It is not fun to worry. Typical Agile is an enticing antidote to worry, in its escalation of "detailed planning is not worth it" to a first-class citizen.

It is also true that because planning is a cross-functional process, each team that has input has a different and incomplete set of worries. Product managers do not always understand deeper engineering concerns. Developers do not always think about what makes sense from a customer experience or market perspective. QE focuses more on how a feature would be used or tested, not necessarily how it would or should be designed. They know that they cannot plan in detail for the future simply by virtue of the fact that they, alone, do not know everything they need to know.

Because of this, and the siloing that typical Agile processes put on these teams, there is little experience to draw on to say from any individual perspective that detailed planning could be easy or worthwhile. It has never been done as a group at any distance beyond a sprint boundary.

This challenge is also the great opportunity that the Agile Codex method presents. The first few grooming sessions are awkward. PM and UX may not bring enough detail. Developers may not be accustomed to thinking of their AC in such detail, or of their work being constructed as an independent, executable unit in terms of dependencies in relation to other work also being created at the same time.

But these muscles do grow. And quickly.

With regard to the concern of meeting overload, I have seen repeatedly that within a few months, each of my teams has exercised this methodology to the point at which we can optimize the information each party brings to the grooming session, and what type of grooming session is appropriate at which stage.

Typically, initial grooming happens in person as questions are refined and assumptions are challenged. User Stories are groomed asynchronously, over Slack, with explicit sign-off required from each participant before work can begin. If questions come up during that grooming which would benefit from an ad hoc meeting, it happens quickly and efficiently. The conversation – the "why did we decide this" is archived in Slack, and the result – the "what did we decide" is solidified in the AC of the User Story.

The ultimate point is, we get good at it. It is not slow or cumbersome. Each stakeholder is a contributor and co-owner in the delivery of the work from the beginning to the end, with a vested interest in making their lives *easier* by being involved up-front. This level and type of interaction drives the teams to become good at speaking a common language and speaking with each other. There is no throwing anything over a wall, and no one can ever claim they were on the wrong side of a wall which, in our case, does not exist.

As we execute on the plan, and revisit the planning, each party has a common frame of reference and history of communication with respect to the plan. Everyone on the team sees the others' perspectives and input saving them from nasty surprises, scope creep, edge cases, and missed deadlines. People begin speaking a common language for a common purpose.

Agiling Well with Others When They Don't Agile As Well

As your team becomes the proverbial well-oiled machine, you will start to notice that you no longer have the aches and pains you used to have. There is no more adversarial interaction between teams. There is no more defensive positioning, pressuring, or finger-pointing. The teams speak with one voice, and data replaces anecdotes.

This will probably not be the case for other teams you interact with. You may need to deliver to them or will need to rely on them to deliver to you. You may need to compare your metrics and methods with theirs. You may need to translate your output to whatever common metrics your program managers use to roll up your status.

Over time, your ability to absorb their unpredictability, and to deliver more predictably, will build organizational trust in your team, and whatever asterisks you need to carry along with metrics translations will be met with curiosity rather than rejection.

The most important lesson of all is to listen to everyone. When another team is less predictable, this does not mean their processes are worse. They could have challenges of personalities, skills, resourcing, and more, which you do not have. Take these opportunities to learn and adapt and prepare for the inevitable time when you, too, will have these challenges. You and your teams will also be armed with an expertise in the Agile Codex which will give you a unique position from which to address them.

Which brings us to the final point. The Agile Codex began as a small set of steps encompassing specific practices for a specific organization and a specific project at a specific point in time. Only through talking with, working with, and depending on others, did it grow into a statement of practices that could be separated into more universal principles. We asked ourselves why it was working. And when something else worked better, we adapted our practices and refined our principles. We are still doing this today.

What Next?

Easing the Easy

The common thread in most advice and critique I receive is around the apparent complexity of managing the dependency tree from the tooling available. The theory behind the dependency tree is not simple. The practice of optimizing the tree using the Gantt generation tool presents a significant technical barrier to many project managers who may not be software developers themselves.

The second category of critique lies in the resistance to what appears on the surface as process overhead and the inertia around and resistance to process change as each organization differs from the practical examples I provide. While this book is an endeavor to elaborate and underscore the principles which are most important, leaving room for an infinite expression of practices, it is not possible to write an infinitely long book of examples. So, I will instead give some thoughts to how we can think about the principles themselves, and progressively iterate toward the Agile Codex method in a low-risk way, both culturally and organizationally.

Tooling

The answer to both difficulties starts with tooling. I have found it easiest during the development of the theory to use the spreadsheet-based generation tool. I enjoy the repetitive literalness of cell formulas, and because I understand

M. McCormick, *The Agile Codex*, https://doi.org/10.1007/978-1-4842-7280-0_19

the theory of what it is trying to do (and because I wrote it), I can also easily tweak it as I get better ideas.

At this point, I also almost intuitively understand the heuristics around sequencing and assignment to get to the optimal dependency tree. It does not take me many iterations to get to the plan and to adjust the plan. During a typical release cycle, I refresh the chart once a day, make a couple of tweaks at a time, if necessary, and move on. This process is usually less than ten minutes.

I have not used a project management tool which does this tree generation. The process for using existing and powerful tools such as Jira involves exporting .csv files, sorting them, and pasting them into the data area of the Gantt generator. Tweaks to sequencing and assignments made in the Gantt then need to be manually performed in Jira to keep them synchronized – as Jira is the source of truth and board that the engineers work from.

There are also times, especially early in learning the process, when software developers do not structure or maintain the status of their work according to the principles. The grooming process helps influence the structuring in the right direction, and that disconnect has always been short-lived.

As for maintenance, the Agile Codex flow diagram is a great help in distilling responsibilities and has evolved from the need to address process drift in individual engineers over time. But there are always some who simply do not maintain the level of User Story and board hygiene for which the Codex asks.

After generating the tree, it is not difficult to see these hygiene outages because they most often surface as unanticipated gaps in the plan and calendar / effort drift caused by unidentified dependencies or mis-sequenced work. The conversations I have had with the developers when these occur are largely responsible for the efficiency and low overhead of the process as it exists today, as I have iteratively adapted it to be as practically useful as possible in response to their implicit objections.

Both from the perspective of the management and the maintenance of the tree and plan over time, there is no question that there is a lot of room to continue reducing this overhead, and to create feedback loops in the tooling itself to help everyone execute and maintain their work with low overhead and alignment.

Moving forward, I can imagine a Jira plug-in to close the iteration and synchronization gap by eliminating the export / import step and the manual work to affect Gantt changes back to the tooling source of truth. This plug-in would also manage the complexity of applying optimization heuristics to play out and choose between scenarios. Lastly, it would generate useful metrics and reporting, such as the "calendar time / customer value delivered" charts discussed in Chapter 17, "Metrics."

Synchronization Gap

A plug-in which can directly interact with the project's core data store would be able to obtain the latest source-of-truth at any time. Provisional updates could be made in the plug-in interface until a scenario is chosen, at which time a transactional update to the core data store could be applied.

These provisional updates could take the form of differences from the core representation, much as a historical, materialized snapshot view would be used.

Using this snapshot approach, multiple points in time could also be stored, reconstructed, and compared with other materializations at any time.

From a user experience perspective, this would remove the export / import step and manual synchronization work, and which in turn would eliminate the risk of errors during manual synchronization steps in either direction.

Heuristics

Blindly iterating through all scenarios in order to optimize a large project would be mind-numbing for a human. Even a CPU which probably does not feel those particular emotions would suffer from the time-intensive nature of the work. Additionally, in most projects there will be a fair number of equivalently optimal scenarios. The perfect optimum would not be able take into account external factors which an algorithm cannot know.

I have found myself using a fair number of basic heuristics, though, which could be provided to an optimizer as metadata for a rules engine.

Who Can Do What

The plug-in should be able to match User Stories to developers who are qualified to work on them:

- A taxonomy of skill areas, either fixed or dynamic, should be constructed and managed by the system.

- Allow User Stories to be characterized according to the skill areas they relate to.

- Allow software developers to be labeled according to the skill areas they have expertise and interest in.

- Allow software developers to also opt out of receiving work in certain areas.

- In addition to skill area, allow skill metadata to also indicate and optimize matches based on the skill level of the User Story and software developer.

Risk Ranking

The plug-in should allow a scoring or ranking of User Stories based on technical risk criteria attached to the User Stories.

How Perfect Is Perfect Enough?

Depending on the amount of opportunistic work available, compromises which optimize efficiency may also allow a certain number of gaps.

- Allow User Stories to be indicated as opportunistic.

Who Is Available, How Much, and When?

- Allow software developers to indicate planned time off.

- System should account for limited availability of software developers during company holidays and weekends.

- Allow one to set percentage availability of a given developer over a given amount of time or set of times.

- Factor in availability when scheduling work.

Dials and Knobs for Scenario Planning

Different weightings with respect to specialization, gap allowability, deadline strictness, and risk will generate different optimized scenarios.

Make It Easy to Visualize

It should be simple to see what optimizations contributed to a given scenario in order to apply the "last mile" of human heuristic in the final choice.

Reporting

Reporting functionality of this tooling should support everything defined in Chapter 17, "Metrics," most importantly:

- Snapshots should allow for complete rewind and replay of alternate scenarios.

- Between two snapshots, explore customer value delivered versus calendar time versus scope cut. Changes should be auditable on any and all of those axes.

Additionally:

- Changes in commitment dates should be trackable.

- Requirements escape is surfaced by the creation of a Child User Story during QE and PM / UX Review phases. These should be trackable.

- Quality escape is surfaced by the creation of a Child Bug during QE and PM / UX Review phases. These should be trackable.

Lastly, User Story life cycle is more than just DEV work. Time-to-close through QE and PM / UX Review should also be measured and accounted for. While PM / UX Review is relatively lightweight, QE can be more involved and must be balanced with other, asynchronous QE work such as automation, broad product integration testing, and other QE project initiatives. Ideally, QE would be tracking QE work using the Agile Codex method as applied to QE projects, and would emit compatible signals directly to the same system of record.

In all project tracking systems, not only is quantity at a snapshot useful information, even more important is measuring change in quantities over time, and the change in the change as well. Understanding the direction gives the opportunity to monitor and alert on possibly impactful deviations and areas for improvement. It also implicitly normalizes some of the qualitative measures that go into translation of reality to metrics over time.

Conclusion

There are a myriad of ways a project management approach can serve the principles of the Agile Codex. I have provided a sample of what has worked for me, explaining at each step how that practical approach serves the principles.

At its core, the Agile Codex is two things:

- An industrial engineering lens on the planning, structuring, and execution of software development work.

- Methods of collaboration to achieve this which encourage strong cross-team relationships.

Both of those ingredients, together, ensure that as changes occur during the software development life cycle, a team can respond with agility, optimally minimizing uncertainty and risk, seeing clearly the downstream effects of changes, and responding transparently in the work plan.

The distribution of responsibility, the clear ownership at each stage, and the democratic process around state transitions makes this apparently complex system uniquely powerful and lightweight in practice, with incredibly powerful effects on the skills of each team with respect to planning, working together, and learning to speak with one voice.

> *What would you say you… do here?*
>
> —The Bobs, *Office Space*

As I have moved in my career from individual contributor to manager (and back and forth a few times), I have always felt uniquely vulnerable as a manager. When one writes code, one can point directly at the thing one has created. There is no ambiguity. Things are less clear for managers.

M. McCormick, *The Agile Codex*, https://doi.org/10.1007/978-1-4842-7280-0

The ultimate rubric is the trust that a project manager instills in the teams they manage and in the organization as a whole. There is no stronger path to trust than to provide total transparency with insight. The Agile Codex makes this transparency simple, the output more predictable, and the cost of change so measurable that there is no ambiguity when cross-organization buy-in, explanation, or nuance is needed.

There is nothing more effective to instilling trust than to have a quick answer, at any level, in the present as to what is, and a quick answer, at any level, retrospectively as to how it got there. To be able to do this with such a lightweight process has been life and career changing, and this is just the beginning.

My hope is that as this process is adopted by the community of software developers, we can evolve it, together, building out ever more sophisticated tooling and broadening the pool of experience when applying it to all manner of environments and situations to hone and optimize and intelligently refine the usefulness of the approach.

Index

A

Acceptable risk, 139

Acceptance criteria (AC), 27, 38, 48, 102, 104

Acyclic dependency tree, 51, 53, 84, 114, 116

Adjacent teams, 103, 117

Agile approaches, 98, 143

Agile Codex
  application, 54, 55
  benefits, 61
    detailed auditing, 62
    low overhead, 62
    many quality gates, 63
    quick and safe deliveries, 63
  collaboration and alignment of
      interests, 57
  definition, 51
  inputs, 58
  outputs, 59
  ownership of work, 58
  parameters, dependency tree nodes, 55
  practice principles 57
    clear inputs, 58
    clear outputs, 59
    clear transition criteria, 58
    detailed auditing, 62
    low overhead, 61, 62
    many quality gates, 63
    quick and safe deliveries, 63
    single owner, 58
    single owner principle, 58
    stakeholder approval, 59

  principles
    acyclic dependency tree, 53
    sequenceable, 53
    short units of work, 52
    single owner, 54
    sized, 53
  stakeholder approval, 59
  steps, 51
  transition, 58

Assembly line
  actions of ordered stages, 68
  constraints, 72
  cost of change, 67
  delaying, shaper and threader
      constructing cylinder, 74
  delaying, shaper and threader
      constructing lid, 73
  delaying, shaper constructing
      cylinder, 72
  imagine backward, 68
  ordered stages, 68
  physical components, 67
  sequencing alternatives, 74
  tools and actions of ordered stages, 69
  transformation time, 69
  waiting, 70, 71

B

Blast radius comparison, 19

Broken life cycle, 21, 22

Bug, 3, 16, 66, 102, 104

M. McCormick, *The Agile Codex*, https://doi.org/10.1007/978-1-4842-7280-0

Building blocks
AC, 102
adjacent teams, 103
bug, 104
dependencies, 103
epic, 102
ERD, 105
high-level rules, 101
planned release, 102
story points, 104
tasks, 103
user story, 102
Business risks, 88, 89

C

Cadence, 80, 81, 105, 130
Calendar time, 32
Code review, simplifying, 18
Context switching, 31, 32, *See also*
Interruptions
Cross-team and cross-functional
dependencies, 114
Cultural template, 58
Customer support group (CSG), 78
Cyclic dependency, 32

D

Death by ambiguity, 11
Dependencies, 32, 33
Dependency management, 143, 144
Development (DEV), 78
Discovered scope, 140
Documentation (DOC), 78

E, F

Effort time, 32, 48
Engineering management (EM), 78
Epic, 102, 108, 109, 112
Epic commitment, 109, 118, 119
Epic grooming, 109, 114–116
External dependencies, 128–130

G

Gantt chart, 120, 140
Gantt generation tool, 147
Gating factor, 70
Grooming, 108, 109, 145
Grooming line, 110, 111

H

Heuristics, 148, 149

I, J

Interruptions, 18, 27
costs of disconnects, 22
ownership disconnected from, 21
Iterative grooming, 113

K

Kanban, 81, 130

L

Learned helplessness, 26
Life cycle, 22
phase change rules, 35
phase transition, 38, 39, 61
stakeholder approval, 38
replanning, 47
transition criteria, 34, 35, 37
Lightweight process, 154
Locality, 38
Local knowledge, 9

M

Market risk, 88
Merge conflicts
branch life cycle, 16
code reviews, 17
experimental branch, 17
logic/semantic changes, 16
vectors, 16
Metrics
adjusting, 140, 141

ambiguity, 136
analyzing, 138–140
deed, recording and deciding, 137
fidelity, 135
high fidelity, 135
multi-release epics, 142
opportunistic and non-epic work,
    141, 142
planning and execution, 135
predicting, 137, 138
Minimum Viable Product, 66
Multi-conveyor-belt-like Kanban approach, 81
Multi-release epics, 142

N

Non-epic work, 141, 142

O

Operations (OPS), 78
Organizational reporting chart, 10
Ownership
    accountability, establishing
        through, 10
    plausible deniability, 10
    problem of shared, 9
    process, establishing through, 10
    volunteers, reliance on, 10

P

Phase transition, 38, 39, 61
Planned release, 102
Planning
    building the muscles of, 32
    execution balance, 107
    grooming, 108, 109
    learned helplessness, 26
    muscle of, 32
    phases of delivery, 110
    purpose of sizing, 29
    resilience, 93–97
Product management (PM), 77, 127
Product risk, 81, 88
Project management tool, 148

Q

Quality engineering (QE), 78, 127
Quality gates, 21, 63, 127
Quick and safe deliveries, 63

R

Regression, blast radius, 19, 20
Regression risk, 18
Release planning, 109–114
Reporting functionality, 151
Requirements escape, 140
Resilience
    effort types, 93
    failure mitigation, 95
    failure recovery, 96, 97
    independent and uncompleted work, 94
Risk, 46, 47
Risk management
    categories
        business risk, 88
        market risk, 88
        product risk, 88
        technical risk, 88
    invention, 89
    planned transformations, 98
    planning for resilience, 93–97
    prioritizing, 98
    quadrants, 91, 92
    resilience, 93
    through time, 90
    today and tomorrow risk, 89
Risk minimization, 140
Risk mitigation, 97
Risk ranking, 150

S

Scenario planning, 150
Scope of work, 16
    importance of keeping small, 15
Scope creep, 140
Shared lists
    personal perspective, 7

Single owner principle, 58

Sizing, 26, 27
   change in, 26
   total lifetime of a User Story, 47

Software development life cycle (SDLC)
   cadence, 80, 81
   constructing the Codex, 84, 85
   inter-cycle planning, 83
   phases, 80
      execution, 80
      planning, 80
      releasing, 80
   product risk, 81
   release Agile time allocations, 82, 83
   re-planning, 83
   Sprint Agile, 82
   Sprint Agile time allocations, 82
   sprint-based Agile, 82
   technical risk, 81
   up-front planning, 83
   waterfall, 81

Sprints/Kanban, 82, 83, 130, 131

Stack ranking, 112

Stakeholder approval, 38, 59, 61

State transitions, 153

Story grooming, 109, 116–118

Story points, 104

Synchronization gap, 149

T

Tasks, 84, 103, 109

Teams
   from Agile to Agile Codex, 144–146
   anecdotes, 146
   cross-team and cross-functional
      dependencies, 144
   data *vs.* anecdotes, 146
   dependency management, 144
   organizational trust, 146

Technical risk, 81, 82, 88

Terminal sprint, 133

to-do lists, 3
   as User Stories, 3
   single-owner input/output life cycle, 11
   unphased shared to-dos, 11

Tooling, 147, 148
   heuristics, 148
      matching developers to work
        items, 147
      risk ranking, 150
   reporting

U

Uncertainty, 153

Unpredictable delivery times, 31

User activity logging, 33

User-centric language, 117

User experience (UX), 77, 127

User story, 102

User Story grooming, 108, 115, 116, 117

V

Velocity, 137, 138

Visualization, 120, 150

W, X, Y

Waterfall, 81, 144

Work backlog, 49

Workflow
   accounting, 132
   accounting for offset, 132
   adjusting, 131
   board, 125, 128
   changing assignee, 124
   changing scope, 125
   changing sequence, 123
   child attribute, 122
   closed, 128
   epic commitment, 118, 119
   epic grooming, 114–116
   execution, setting up tree, 119, 120, 122,
      123, 125
   external dependencies, 128–130
   feature complete, 131, 132
   fix needed, 126
   planning, 107–109
   PM/UX, 127
   principles, 107
   in progress, 126
   QE, 127

QE complete, 132
release planning, 110–114, 131
sequence of work, 121
signed off, 126
sprints/Kanban, 130, 131
story grooming, 116–118
story points, 120, 121
terminal sprint, 133

Workflow state buffer, 46
Work parallelization, 30
Work qualification, 149

Z

Zero bug metric, 132

Printed in the United States
by Baker & Taylor Publisher Services